STUDENT NOTES FOR DIGITAL LESSONS

Grade 4

NAME _____

© 2023 Zearn

Portions of this work, Zearn Math, are derivative of Eureka Math and licensed by Great Minds. © 2019 Great Minds. All rights reserved.

Zearn® is a registered trademark.

Printed in the U.S.A.

10 9 8 7 6 5 4 3 2 1

ISBN: 979-8-88868-891-5

GRADE 4 – CONTENTS

Mission 1	Add, Subtract, and Round	5
Mission 2	Measure and Solve	37
Mission 3	Multiply and Divide Big Numbers	49
Mission 4	Construct Lines, Angles, and Shapes	101
Mission 5	Equivalent Fractions	129
Mission 6	Decimal Fractions	193
Mission 7	Multiply and Measure	219

Grade 4

Mission 1
Add, Subtract, and Round

Lesson 1
G:4 M:1

Bundle Action!
ZEARN STUDENT NOTES

Name:_____ Date:_____

Complete: ☐ Class:_____

1 Label the place value chart. Fill in the blanks to make the following equations true. Draw disks in the place value chart to show how your got your answer, using arrows to show any bundling.

10 × 3 ones = _____ ones = _____ _____

7

EXTRA WORKSPACE

Nicolaus

Lesson 2
G:4 M:1

10 Times

ZEARN STUDENT NOTES

Name:_____ Date:_____

Complete: ☐ Class:_____

1 Label the place value chart. Then, represent the quotient by drawing disks on the place value chart.

2 thousands ÷ 10 = _____ hundreds ÷ 10 = _____

EXTRA WORKSPACE

Lesson 3
G:4 M:1

Commas,
ZEARN STUDENT NOTES

Name:_____ Date:_____

Complete: ☐ Class:_____

1 Rewrite the number below including commas where appropriate.

6 0 8 4 3 0 3 2 5 = _____

2 Write these units in standard form. Be sure to place commas where appropriate.

4 ten thousands 7 thousands 2 hundreds 4 ones = _____

hundred thousands	ten thousands	thousands	hundreds	tens	ones

EXTRA WORKSPACE

Lesson 4
G:4 M:1

What's Your Name?
ZEARN STUDENT NOTES

Name:_____ Date:_____

Complete: ☐ Class:_____

1

a. On the place value chart below, label the units and represent the number 36,094.

b. Write the number in expanded form.

_____

c. Write the number in word form.

_____

EXTRA WORKSPACE

Lesson 5
G:4 M:1

<, >, or =?
ZEARN STUDENT NOTES

Name:_____ Date:_____

Complete: ☐ Class:_____

1 Label the units in the place value chart. Draw place value disks to represent each number in the place value chart. Use <, >, or = to compare the two numbers. Write the correct symbol in the circle.

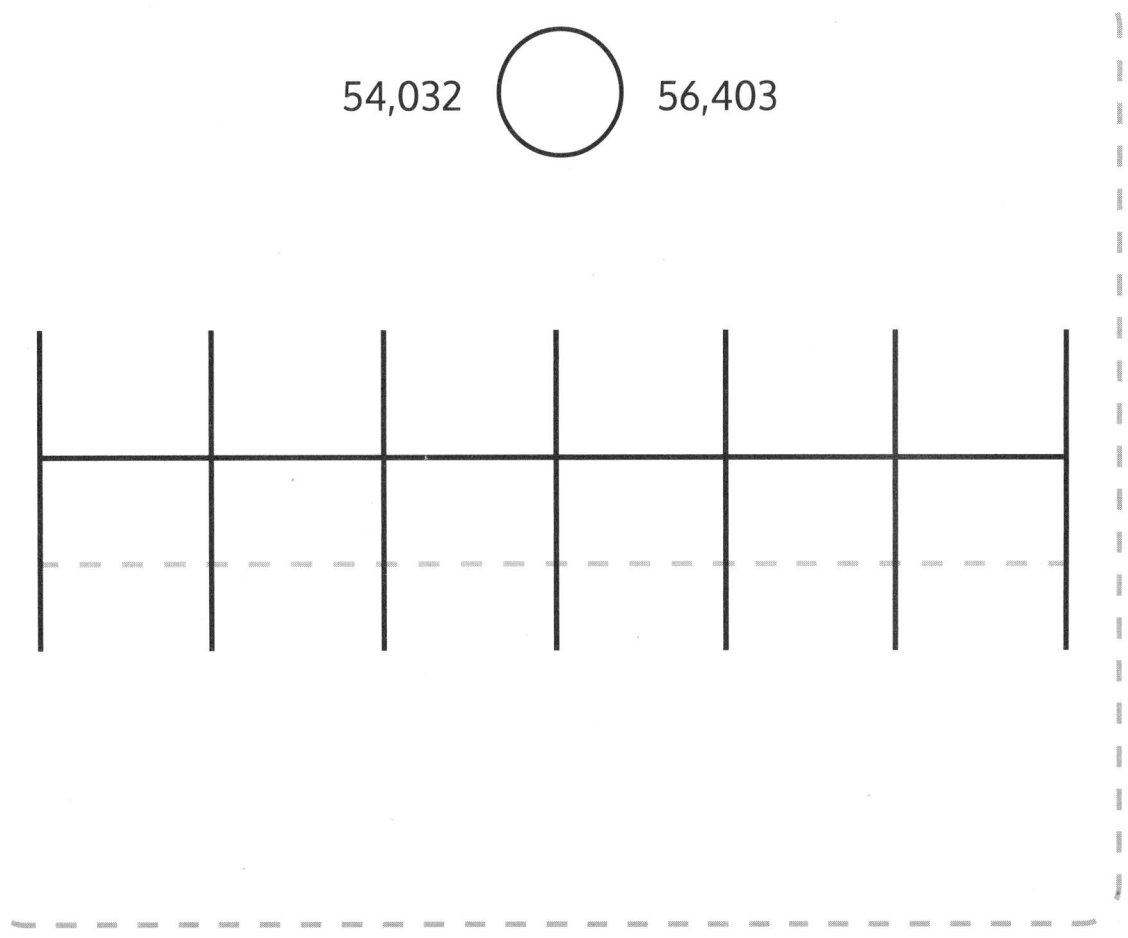

15

EXTRA WORKSPACE

Lesson 7
G:4 M:1

Round and Round
ZEARN STUDENT NOTES

Name:_____ Date:_____

Complete: ☐ Class:_____

1 Round to the nearest thousand. Use the number line to model your thinking.

23,500 ≈ _____

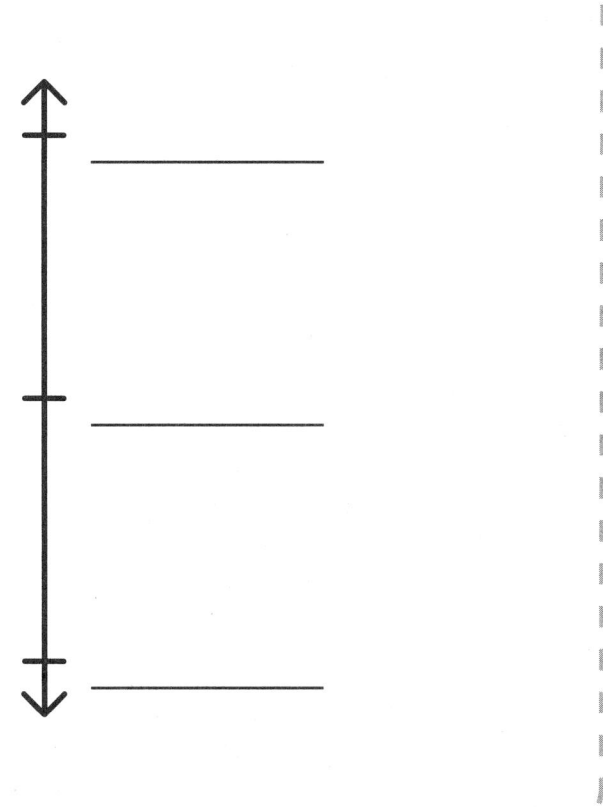

EXTRA WORKSPACE

Lesson 8
G:4 M:1

Oh, the Places You'll Round!

ZEARN STUDENT NOTES

Name:_____ Date:_____

Complete: ☐ Class:_____

1 Complete the statement by rounding the number to the given place value. Use the number line to show your work.

749,085 rounded to the nearest hundred thousand is _____

EXTRA WORKSPACE

Lesson 10 G:4 M:1	**Round the World**
	ZEARN STUDENT NOTES

Name:_____ Date:_____

Complete: ☐ Class:_____

1 In the year 2012, there were 936,292 visitors to the White House. Assume that the White House provides a map for each visitor.

Use this information to predict the number of White House maps needed for visitors in 2013.

ROUND

Thousand _____

Ten Thousand _____

Hundred Thousand _____

EXPLAIN

_____
_____
_____
_____
_____

 2,837 students attend Lincoln Elementary School.

How would you estimate the number of chairs needed in the school?

ESTIMATE AND EXPLAIN

2,837 ≈ _____

_____

_____

_____

_____

EXTRA WORKSPACE

Lesson 11
G:4 M:1

Add It Up
ZEARN STUDENT NOTES

Name:_____ Date:_____

Complete: ☐ Class:_____

1. A baseball stadium sells burgers. On Friday night, they sold 806 burgers. On Saturday night, they sold 186 more burgers than on Friday.

How many burgers did they sell on Saturday night?

TAPE DIAGRAM

SOLVE

ANSWER SENTENCE

EXTRA WORKSPACE

Lesson 12 G:4 M:1	**Sum Sense**
	ZEARN STUDENT NOTES

Name:_____   Date:_____

Complete: ☐   Class:_____

1. On Saturday, 32,736 more movie tickets were sold than on Sunday. On Sunday, only 17,295 tickets were sold.

How many people bought movie tickets over the weekend?

DRAW

Sunday

Saturday

SOLVE

There were _____ tickets sold over the weekend.

 Last year, Big Bill's Department Store sold many pairs of shoes: 118,214 pairs of boots were sold; 37,092 more pairs of sandals than pairs of boots were sold; and 124,417 more pairs of sneakers than pairs of boots were sold.

How many pairs of shoes were sold last year?

DRAW

_____

_____

_____

SOLVE

Big Bill's Department Store sold exactly _____ pairs of shoes last year.

Lesson 13
G:4 M:1

Subtraction Action
ZEARN STUDENT NOTES

Name:_____ Date:_____

Complete: ☐ Class:_____

1 During the month of March, 48,025 pounds of king crab were caught.

If 5,614 pounds were caught in the first week of March, how many pounds were caught in the rest of the month?

TAPE DIAGRAM

SUBTRACTION

CHECK YOUR WORK

EXTRA WORKSPACE

Lesson 14 G:4 M:1	Take It Away
	ZEARN STUDENT NOTES

Name:_____   Date:_____

Complete: ☐   Class:_____

1 Mrs. Johnson needed to purchase a large order of computer supplies for her company. She was allowed to spend $859,239 on computers. However, she ended up only spending $272,650.

How much money was left?

TAPE DIAGRAM

SUBTRACTION | CHECK YOUR WORK

ANSWER SENTENCE

EXTRA WORKSPACE

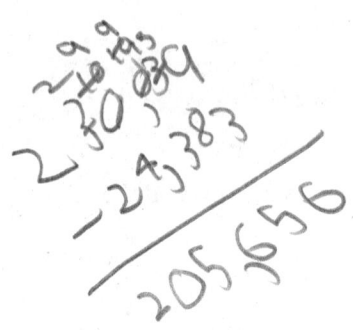

Lesson 16
G:4 M:1

Break It and Tape It
ZEARN STUDENT NOTES

Name:_____ Date:_____

Complete: ☐ Class:_____

1. An amusement park's goal is to sell 1 million tickets within the first four months of its being open. Below is a chart showing the number of tickets sold each month.

How many more tickets does the park need to sell in Month 4 to reach this goal?

Month	Month 1	Month 2	Month 3	Month 4
Tickets	228,211	301,856	299,542	

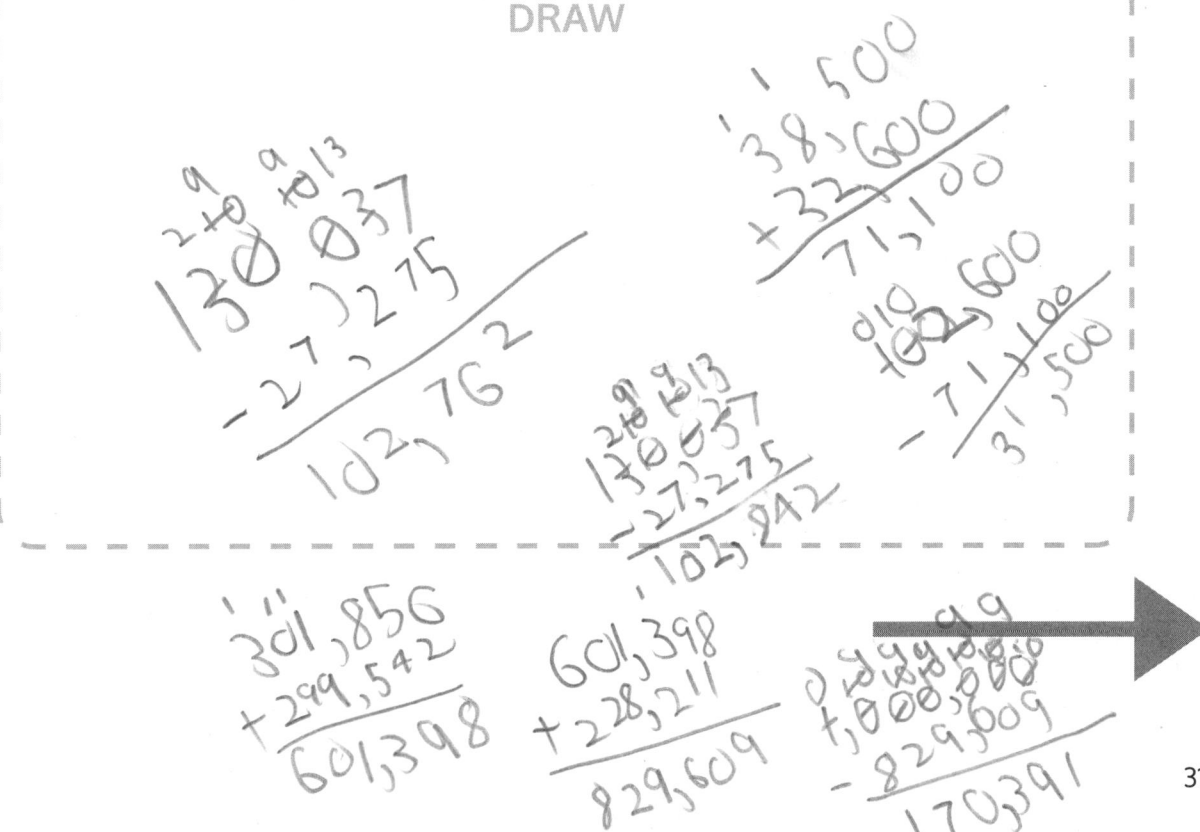

ESTIMATE

SOLVE

The park needs to sell _____ more tickets.

Lesson 18
G:4 M:1

Reflect on Reasonableness
ZEARN STUDENT NOTES

Name:_____ Date:_____

Complete: ☐ Class:_____

1 In one year a factory produced 11,650 gallons of lemonade, 4,950 fewer gallons of iced tea than lemonade, and 3,500 fewer gallons of root beer than iced tea.

How many gallons were produced in all?

DRAW	SOLVE

_____ gallons were produced that year.

2 An ice cream shop sold 12,789 chocolate and 9,324 cookie dough cones. They sold 1,078 more peanut butter cones than cookie dough cones, and 999 more vanilla cones than chocolate cones.

What was the total number of ice cream cones sold?

DRAW

Chocolate

Cookie Dough

Vanilla

Peanut Butter

SOLVE

They sold _____ ice cream cones.

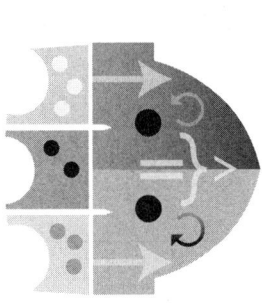

ZEARN

Congratulations!
You completed

Grade 4 Mission 1
Add, Subtract, and Round

 Zearned it!

....
Name

••••••
Date

Grade 4

Mission 2

Measure and Solve

$$\begin{array}{r} \overset{6\ 14}{7\cancel{6},\cancel{7}\cancel{5}\cancel{5}} \\ -44,457 \\ \hline 32,298 \end{array}$$

$$\begin{array}{r} \overset{7\ 14}{6,7\cancel{8}\cancel{4}} \\ -2,048 \\ \hline 4,736 \end{array}$$

Lesson 2
G:4 M:2

Mix and Match
ZEARN STUDENT NOTES

Name:_____ Date:_____

Complete: ☐ Class:_____

1. Solve 25 kg 537 g + 5 kg 723 g using two strategies.

Convert kilograms to grams and add	Add the kilograms and add the grams

2 Solve

10 kg − 2 kg 250 g

SHOW YOUR WORK

EXTRA WORKSPACE

Lesson 3
G:4 M:2

Fluidly Decompose
ZEARN STUDENT NOTES

Name:_____ Date:_____

Complete: ☐ Class:_____

1   32 L 420 mL + 13 L 585 mL

SHOW YOUR WORK

2   12 L 215 mL − 8 L 600 mL

> **SHOW YOUR WORK**
>
> 12 L 215 mL
> − 8 L 600 mL
> ─────────
>
> 8 L 600 mL $\xrightarrow{+\ ?}$ 12 L 215 mL

Lesson 4
G:4 M:2

Like This Like That
ZEARN STUDENT NOTES

Name:_____ Date:_____

Complete: ☐ Class:_____

1 Which is more: 724,706 mL or 72 L 760 mL?

100 L (100,000 mL)	10 L (10,000 mL)	1 L (1,000 mL)	100 mL	10 mL	1 mL

724,706 mL ◯ 72 L 760 mL

43

EXTRA WORKSPACE

Lesson 5
G:4 M:2

Use Your Units
ZEARN STUDENT NOTES

Name:_____ Date:_____

Complete: ☐ Class:_____

1 Adele let out 18 meters and 46 centimeters of string to fly the kite. She then let out 13 meters and 78 centimeters more before reeling back in 590 centimeters.

How much string does Adele still have out?

DRAW

SOLVE

Adele still has _____ m and _____ cm of string out.

2. On Thursday, the pizzeria used 1,888 fewer grams of flour than it used on Friday. On Friday, it used 12 kilograms 240 grams.

What was the total amount of flour used over the two days?

DRAW

SOLVE

The pizzeria used _____ kg _____ g of flour over the two days.

ZEARN

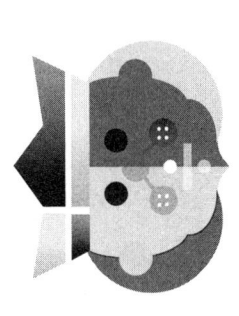

Congratulations!
You completed

Grade 4 Mission 2
Measure and Solve

Zearned it!

Name

Date

Grade 4

Mission 3

Multiply and Divide Big Numbers

Lesson 1
G:4 M:3

In 'n' Out
ZEARN STUDENT NOTES

Name:_____ Date:_____

Complete: ☐ Class:_____

1

9 cm

3 cm

P = _____ A = _____

P = _____ A = _____

P = _____ A = _____

EXTRA WORKSPACE

Lesson 2
G:4 M:3

Dynamic Dimensions

ZEARN STUDENT NOTES

Name:_____ Date:_____

Complete: ☐ Class:_____

1 A rectangle is 2 meters wide. It is 3 times as long as it is wide.

a. Draw a diagram of the rectangle and label its dimensions.

b. Find the perimeter and area of the rectangle

P = _____ A = _____

P = _____ A = _____

P = _____ A = _____

53

EXTRA WORKSPACE

Lesson 3
G:4 M:3

As Long, As Wide
ZEARN STUDENT NOTES

Name:_____ Date:_____

Complete: ☐ Class:_____

The projection screen in the school auditorium is 3 times as long and 3 times as wide as the screen in the library. The screen in the library is 3 meters long with a perimeter of 10 meters.

1. What is the perimeter of the screen in the auditorium? What is the area of each screen?

DRAW

SOLVE

P = _____ P = _____

A = _____ A = _____

55

2 Compare the perimeter of the two screens.

Compare the area of the two screens.

PERIMETER

AREA

EXTRA WORKSPACE

Lesson 4
G:4 M:3

Leftward Ho
ZEARN STUDENT NOTES

Name:_____ Date:_____

Complete: ☐ Class:_____

1 Use a simplifying strategy to solve 4 × 500.

SHOW YOUR WORK

4 × 500

= 4 × (5 × _____)

= (4 × _____) × 100

= 20 × _____

= (_____ × _____) × 100

= 2 × (_____ × _____)

= 2 × _____

= _____

EXTRA WORKSPACE

Lesson 6
G:4 M:3

Free Associate
ZEARN STUDENT NOTES

Name:_____ Date:_____

Complete: ☐ Class:_____

1 Use an area model to solve 50 × 40.

AREA MODEL

SHOW YOUR WORK

_____ tens × _____ tens = _____ _____

50 × 40 = _____

EXTRA WORKSPACE

Lesson 8 G:4 M:3	Twice Is Nice
	ZEARN STUDENT NOTES

Name:_____   Date:_____

Complete: ☐   Class:_____

1 Represent the following expression with disks, regrouping as necessary. Solve using the place value chart, then record the partial products vertically.

3 × 763

thousands	hundreds	tens	ones

        _____
    ×   ____
        _____

EXTRA WORKSPACE

Lesson 9 G:4 M:3	Twinsies!
	ZEARN STUDENT NOTES

Name:_____ Date:_____

Complete: ☐   Class:_____

1 Represent the following expression with disks, regrouping as necessary. Solve using the place value chart, then the algorithm.

6 × 162

hundreds	tens	ones

_____
× _____
_____

63

EXTRA WORKSPACE

Lesson 11
G:4 M:3

Area of Interest
ZEARN STUDENT NOTES

Name:_____ Date:_____

Complete: ☐ Class:_____

1 A cafeteria makes 4,408 lunches each day.

How many lunches are made Monday through Friday?

SHOW YOUR WORK

65

EXTRA WORKSPACE

Lesson 12
G:4 M:3

All for One, One for All
ZEARN STUDENT NOTES

Name:_____ Date:_____

Complete: ☐ Class:_____

1. The Turner family uses 548 liters of water per day. The Hill family uses 3 times as much water per day.

How much water does the Hill family use per week?

DRAW

SOLVE

2 The table shows the cost of party favors. Each party guest receives a bag with 1 balloon, 1 lollipop, and 1 bracelet.

What is the total cost for 9 guests?

Item	Cost
1 balloon	26 ¢
1 lollipop	14 ¢
1 bracelet	33 ¢

SOLVE

Lesson 13
G:4 M:3

These Times Are No Joke!

ZEARN STUDENT NOTES

Name:_____ Date:_____

Complete: ☐ Class:_____

1. Over the summer, Kate earned $180 each week for 7 weeks. Of that money, she spent $375 on a new computer and $137 on new clothes.

How much money did she have left?

DRAW

Earned [   ]

Spent [   ]

SOLVE

Kate had _____ left.

2 Three boxes weighing 128 pounds each and one box weighing 254 pounds were loaded onto the back of an empty truck. A crate of apples was then loaded onto the same truck.

If the total weight loaded onto the truck was 2,000 pounds, how much did the crate of apples weigh?

DRAW

SOLVE

The crate of apples weighed _____ pounds.

Lesson 14 G:4 M:3	That's What's Left
	ZEARN STUDENT NOTES

Name:_____ Date:_____

Complete: ☐ Class:_____

1 Kristy bought 13 roses.

If she puts 6 roses in each vase, how many vases will she use? Will there be any roses left over?

ARRAY

SHOW YOUR WORK

_____ ÷ _____

The quotient is _____ .

The remainder is _____ .

Kristy will use _____ vases.

There will be _____ rose left over.

2 Use a tape diagram to solve 13 divided by 4.

TAPE DIAGRAM

SOLVE

The quotient is _____ .

The remainder is _____ .

CHECK YOUR WORK

Lesson 16
G:4 M:3

Divisible Disks

ZEARN STUDENT NOTES

Name:_____ Date:_____

Complete: ☐ Class:_____

1 Solve 36 ÷ 3 using the place value chart and division algorithm.

PLACE VALUE CHART

tens	ones

36 ÷ 3 = _____

ALGORITHM

CHECK YOUR WORK

_____ × _____ = _____

EXTRA WORKSPACE

Lesson 17 G:4 M:3	Ten Is Not the End
	ZEARN STUDENT NOTES

Name:_____ Date:_____

Complete: ☐ Class:_____

1   56 ÷ 2

tens	ones

$2\overline{)56}$

quotient = _____

remainder = _____

CHECK YOUR WORK

75

EXTRA WORKSPACE

Lesson 20
G:4 M:3

Break and Build

ZEARN STUDENT NOTES

Name:_____ Date:_____

Complete: ☐ Class:_____

1 Solve 96 ÷ 4 using an area model. Draw a number bond and use the distributive property to solve for the unknown length.

NUMBER BOND

EXTRA WORKSPACE

Lesson 22
G:4 M:3

Two of a Kind

ZEARN STUDENT NOTES

Name:_____ Date:_____

Complete: ☐ Class:_____

1 Record the factors of the given numbers as multiplication sentences and as a list in order from least to greatest. Classify each as prime (P) or composite (C).

	Multiplication Sentences	Factors	Prime (P) or Composite (C)
a.	21	The factors of 21 are:	
b.	5	The factors of 5 are:	

79

EXTRA WORKSPACE

Lesson 24 G:4 M:3	**Mighty Multiples**
	ZEARN STUDENT NOTES

Name:_____ Date:_____

Complete: ☐ Class:_____

1

1	2	3	4	5	6	7	8	9	10
11	12	13	14	15	16	17	18	19	20
21	22	23	24	25	26	27	28	29	30
31	32	33	34	35	36	37	38	39	40
41	42	43	44	45	46	47	48	49	50
51	52	53	54	55	56	57	58	59	60
61	62	63	64	65	66	67	68	69	70
71	72	73	74	75	76	77	78	79	80
81	82	83	84	85	86	87	88	89	90
91	92	93	94	95	96	97	98	99	100

a. When a number is a multiple of 2, what are the possible values for the ones digit? _____

b. When a number is a multiple of 5, what are the possible values for the ones digit? _____

c. What digit do all multiples of 10 have in common?

_____

EXTRA WORKSPACE

Lesson 27
G:4 M:3

Side by Side
ZEARN STUDENT NOTES

Name:_____ Date:_____

Complete: ☐ Class:_____

1 Divide. Use the place value chart to model the problem. Then, solve using the algorithm.

726 ÷ 3

PLACE VALUE CHART	ALGORITHM

EXTRA WORKSPACE

Lesson 28
G:4 M:3

Real World Division
ZEARN STUDENT NOTES

Name: _____ Date: _____

Complete: ☐ Class: _____

1. Divide. Use the place value chart to model the problem. Then, solve using the algorithm.

571 ÷ 5

PLACE VALUE CHART

ALGORITHM

CHECK YOUR WORK

EXTRA WORKSPACE

Lesson 29
G:4 M:3

The Great Divide
ZEARN STUDENT NOTES

Name:_____ Date:_____

Complete: ☐ Class:_____

1 Ellie bought two packs of beads. Altogether she has 1,254 beads.

If the number of beads in each bag is the same, how many beads are in three packs?

TAPE DIAGRAM

SOLVE | ANSWER SENTENCE

There are _____ beads in 3 packs

87

EXTRA WORKSPACE

Lesson 30
G:4 M:3

Zero to Hero
ZEARN STUDENT NOTES

Name:_____ Date:_____

Complete: ☐ Class:_____

1 Solve 4,218 ÷ 3 using the place value chart and division algorithm.

PLACE VALUE CHART

thousands	hundreds	tens	ones

ALGORITHM

3) 4218

89

EXTRA WORKSPACE

Lesson 31
G:4 M:3

Decoding Division
ZEARN STUDENT NOTES

Name:_____ Date:_____

Complete: ☐ Class:_____

1 Dr. Casey has 1,868 milliliters of Medicine T. She poured equal amounts of the medicine into 4 containers.

How many milliliters of medicine are in each container?

DRAW

SOLVE

_____ mL are in each container.

2 Two hundred thirty-two people are driving to a conference.

If each car holds 4 people, including the driver, how many cars will be needed?

DRAW

SOLVE

_____ cars will be needed.

Lesson 32
G:4 M:3

Are You My Remainder?
ZEARN STUDENT NOTES

Name:_____ Date:_____

Complete: ☐ Class:_____

1 We know there are 7 days in a week.

How many weeks are there in 259 days?

```
┌─────────────────────────────────────┐
│              DRAW                   │
│                                     │
│                                     │
│                                     │
├─────────────────────────────────────┤
│              SOLVE                  │
│                                     │
│                                     │
│                                     │
│                                     │
│    There are _____ weeks in 259 days.│
│                                     │
│  Is there a remainder? _____ │
└─────────────────────────────────────┘
```

2 Everyone is given the same number of colored pencils in art class.

If there are 329 colored pencils, and 8 students, how many pencils does each student receive?

DRAW

SOLVE

Each student will receive _____ colored pencils.

Is there a remainder? _____

Lesson 36
G:4 M:3

Area Modeling
ZEARN STUDENT NOTES

Name:_____ Date:_____

Complete: ☐ Class:_____

1 Solve 25 × 32.

Draw an area model first. Then solve using the vertical algorithm.

AREA MODEL	ALGORITHM

95

EXTRA WORKSPACE

Lesson 37
G:4 M:3

The Two Step
ZEARN STUDENT NOTES

Name:_____ Date:_____

Complete: ☐ Class:_____

1 Solve 43 × 67.

Draw an area model first. Then solve using the vertical algorithm.

AREA MODEL	ALGORITHM

EXTRA WORKSPACE

ZEARN

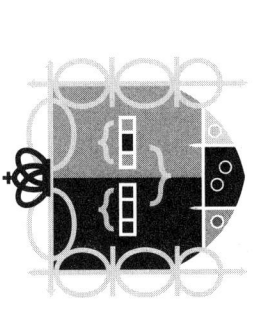

Congratulations!
You completed

Grade 4 Mission 3
Multiply and Divide Big Numbers

Zearned it!

Name .... Date

Grade 4

Mission 4

Construct Lines, Angles, and Shapes

Lesson 1
G:4 M:4

Points, Lines, and Rays! Oh My!
ZEARN STUDENT NOTES

Name:_____ Date:_____

Complete: ☐   Class:_____

1 Plot and connect points to draw $\overline{AB}$, $\overleftrightarrow{AC}$, $\overrightarrow{BD}$, $\overrightarrow{BE}$.

Line segments have _____ endpoints. _____

A line extends in _____ directions without an end. _____

A ray has _____ _____ and goes on forever in one direction. _____

Any _____ _____ sharing the same endpoint create an angle. _____

EXTRA WORKSPACE

Lesson 3
G:4 M:4

Two Lines Make a Right

ZEARN STUDENT NOTES

Name:_____ Date:_____

Complete: ☐ Class:_____

You will need a right angle template or square corner for this lesson.

1 Perpendicular lines intersect to make:

_____ _____

2 Using your right angle template, find and trace right angles in Mr. Sawicki's pictures.

105

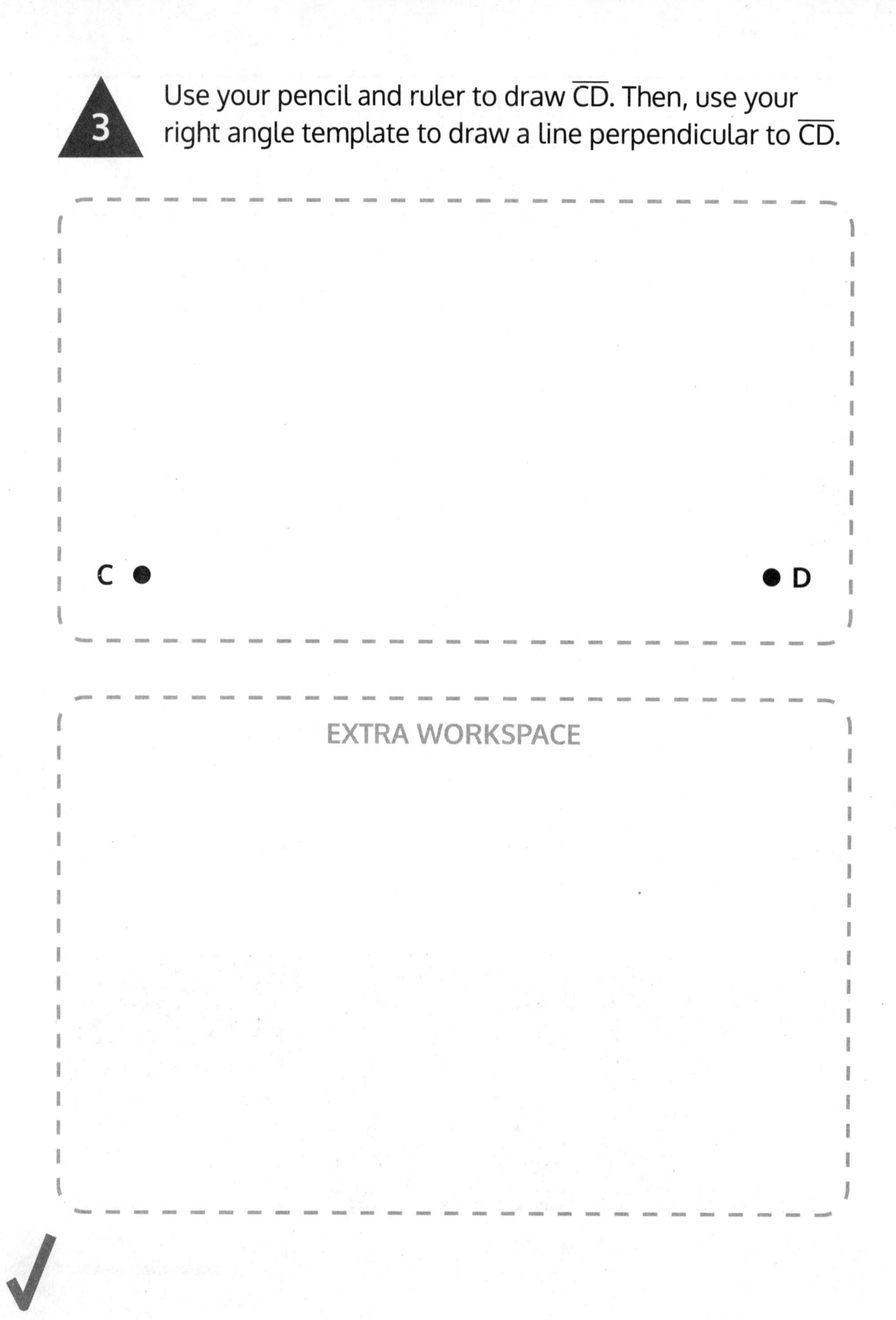

3 Use your pencil and ruler to draw $\overline{CD}$. Then, use your right angle template to draw a line perpendicular to $\overline{CD}$.

C •   • D

EXTRA WORKSPACE

Lesson 4
G:4 M:4

Can't Touch This!
ZEARN STUDENT NOTES

Name:_____ Date:_____

Complete: ☐ Class:_____

You will need a ruler for this lesson.

1 Put your ruler in the drawing area. Then, trace along the two sides of your ruler. Add arrows to the end of your pencil marks.

DRAW

SOLVE

Parallel lines _____ _____

no matter how far you extend them.

2 Using your ruler, find and trace parallel lines in Mr. Sawicki's photos.

Not all of these photos have parallel lines. Mark only the parallel lines that you see.

A   B   C

3 Draw rectangle ABCD on the grid

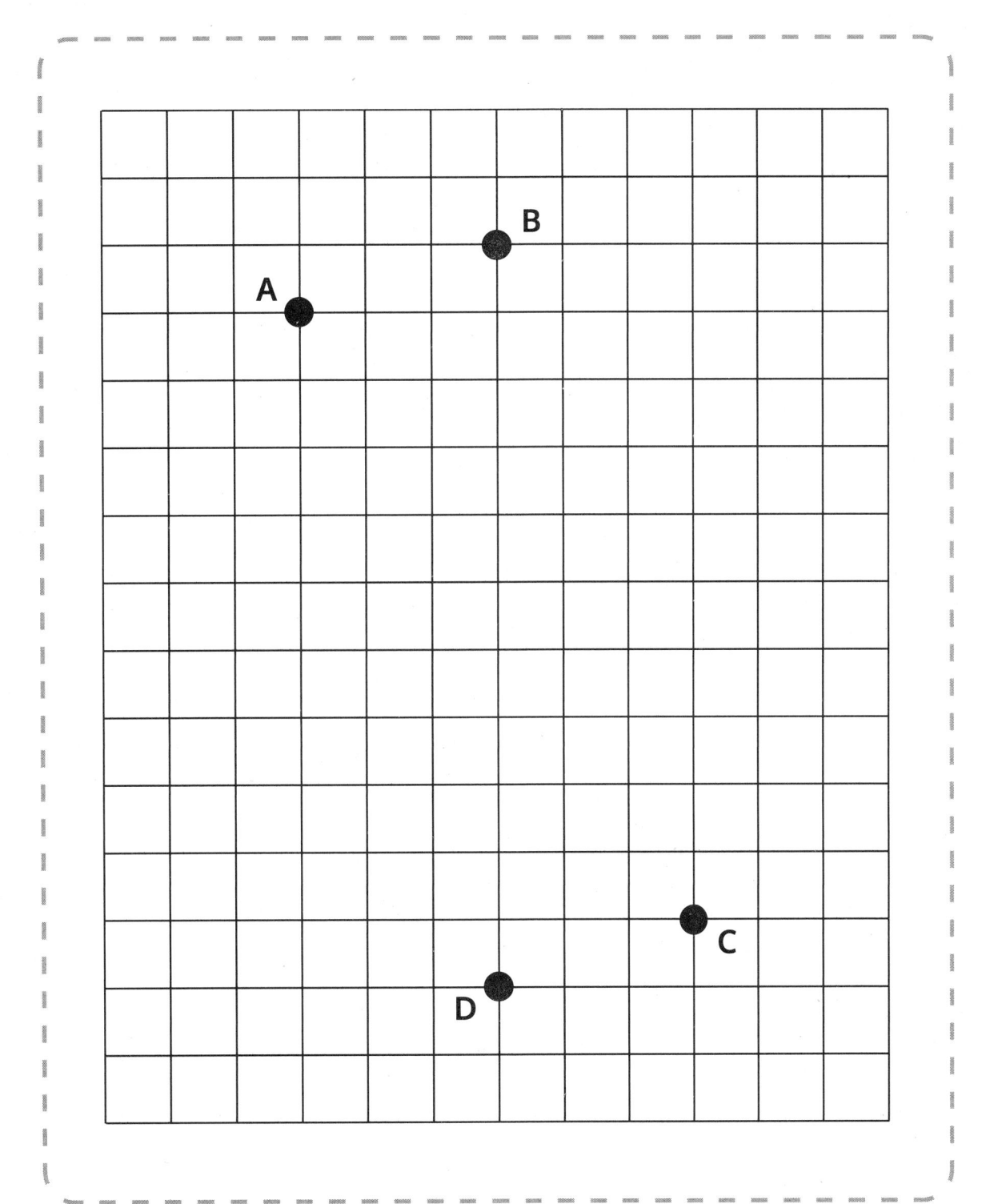

4 Using your straight edge, draw the horizontal line $\overleftrightarrow{XY}$ and parallel line $\overleftrightarrow{ST}$.

X •   Y •

$\overleftrightarrow{XY}$ _____ $\overleftrightarrow{ST}$

EXTRA WORKSPACE

Lesson 6
G:4 M:4

To a Degree
ZEARN STUDENT NOTES

Name:_____ Date:_____

Complete: ☐   Class:_____

1 Use these two protractors to measure angle E.

Protractor 1

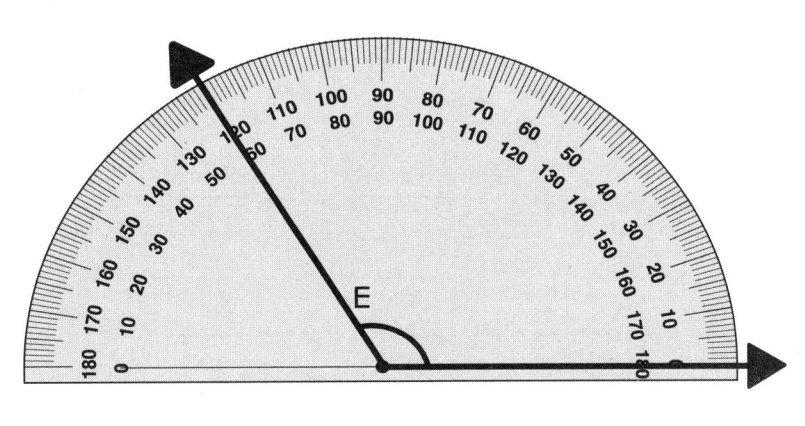

∠E = ____°

Protractor 2

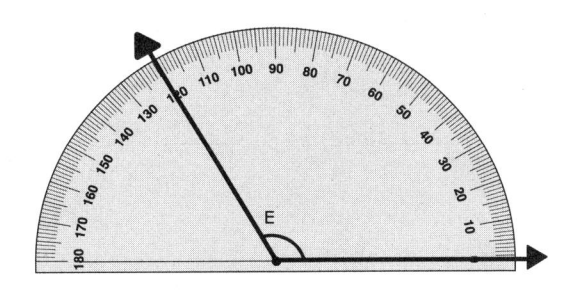

∠E = ____°

111

EXTRA WORKSPACE

Lesson 7
G:4 M:4

Make and Measure
ZEARN STUDENT NOTES

Name:_____ Date:_____

Complete: ☐ Class:_____

You will need a protractor for this lesson.

1 Draw an 80° angle.

DRAWING AREA

2 Draw a 133° angle.

DRAWING AREA

Lesson 8
G:4 M:4

Turn, Turn, Turn
ZEARN STUDENT NOTES

Name:_____ Date:_____

Complete: ☐ Class:_____

1 If Mr. Sawicki makes two quarter turns in the same direction, how many degrees will he have turned?

Mr. Sawicki will have turned _____°.

EXTRA WORKSPACE

Lesson 10 G:4 M:4	The Great Angle Mystery
	ZEARN STUDENT NOTES

Name:_____ Date:_____

Complete: ☐ Class:_____

1 Write a subtraction equation and solve for the unknown angle.

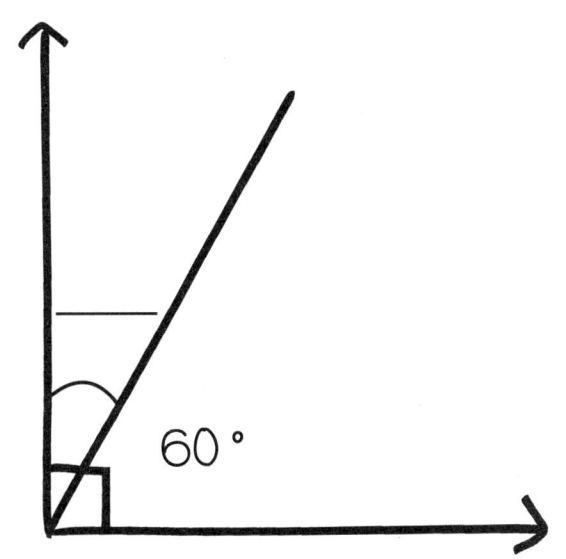

60°

SHOW YOUR WORK

_____ - _____ = _____

Unknown angle = _____°

EXTRA WORKSPACE

Lesson 12
G:4 M:4

So Symmetrical
ZEARN STUDENT NOTES

Name:_____ Date:_____
Complete: ☐ Class:_____

You will need a pair of scissors for this lesson.

1 Use scissors to cut out the shapes on the last page.

2 Look at each image below and determine whether there are any lines of symmetry. If you find any, draw the line that would be created by the fold.

119

3 Use the grid to make a mirror image of the figures that are already drawn.

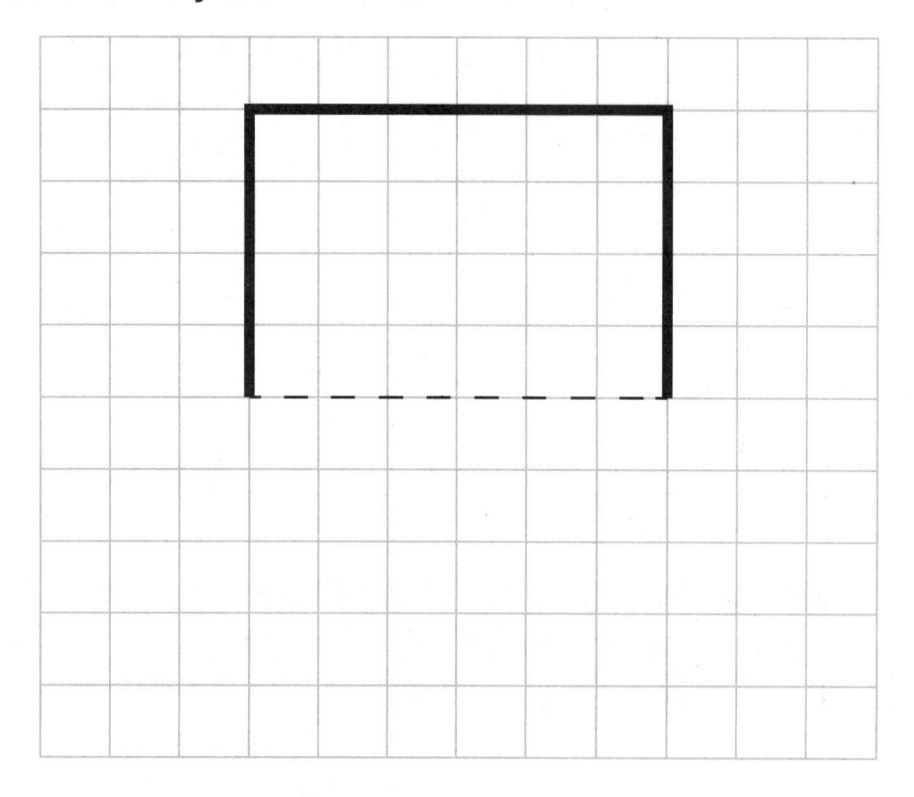

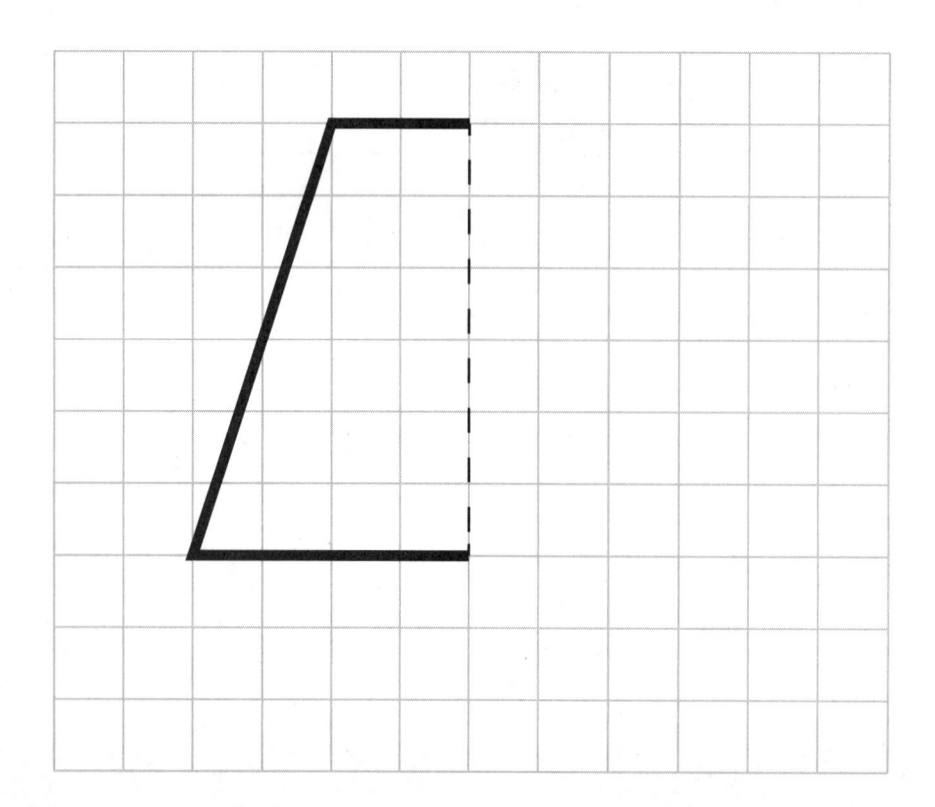

1 Cut the shapes along the dashed lines.

Lesson 13
G:4 M:4

Name That Triangle
ZEARN STUDENT NOTES

Name:_____ Date:_____

Complete: ☐ Class:_____

1 Look at Triangles A - F. Which have no equal sides? 2 equal sides? 3 equal sides?

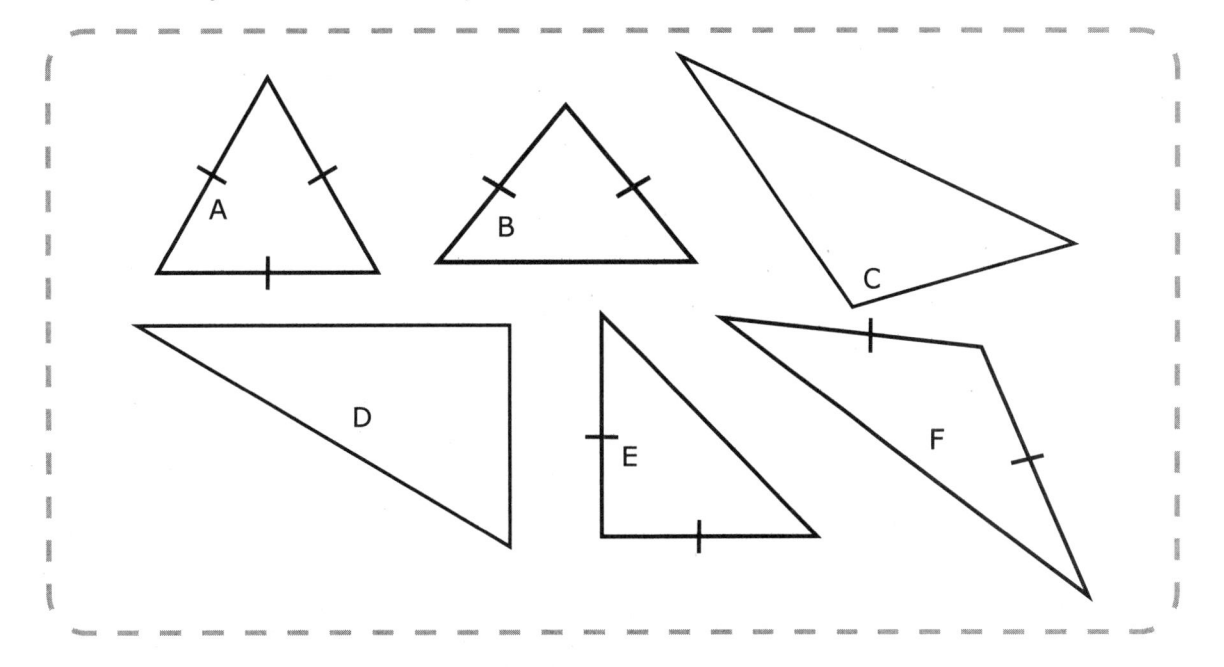

	3 equal sides	2 equal sides	no equal sides
Triangles			

123

2 Use the grid to draw a triangle. Plot three points and label them A, B, and C. Connect the points with line segments to make a triangle.

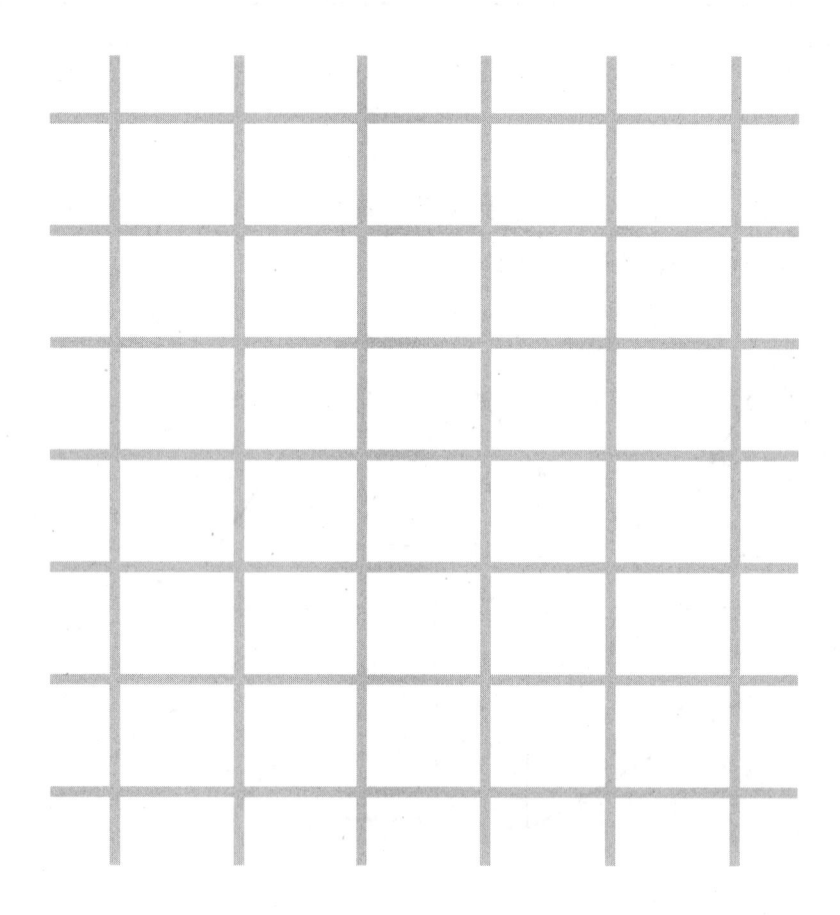

Lesson 15
G:4 M:4

Four Sides — Four Angles
ZEARN STUDENT NOTES

Name:_____ Date:_____

Complete: ☐ Class:_____

You will need a straight edge for this lesson.

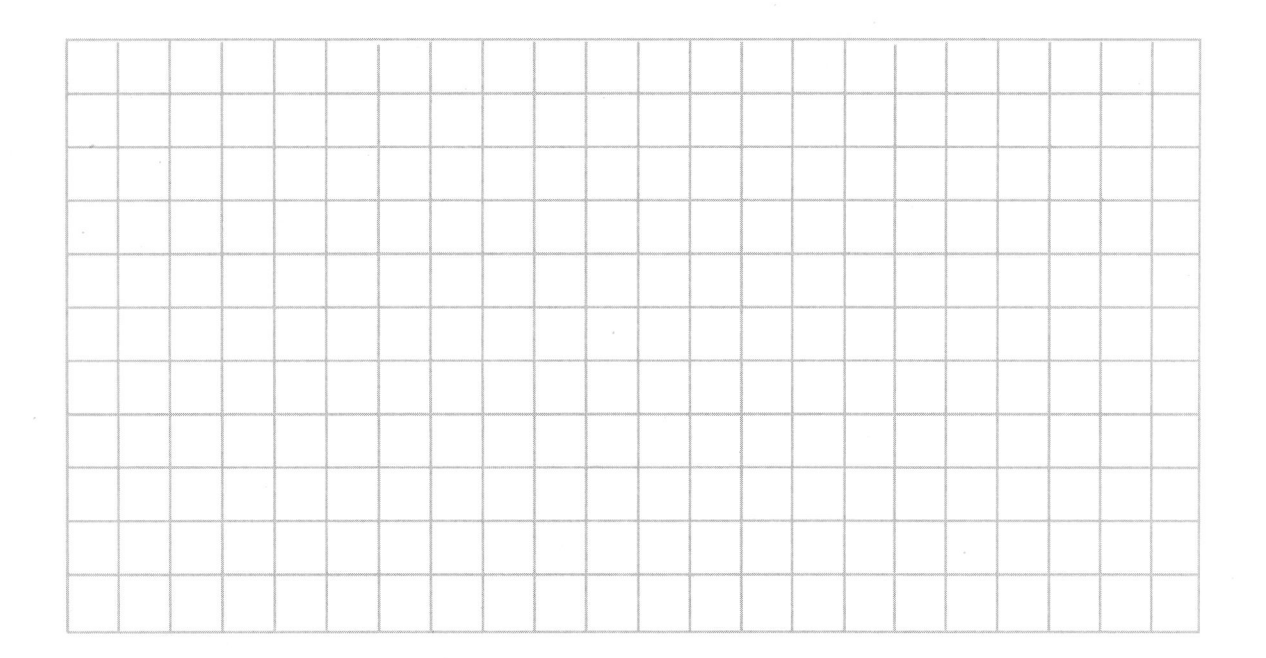

1. Draw a quadrilateral with a least **one** set of parallel sides.

125

2 Draw a quadrilateral with **two** sets of parallel sides.

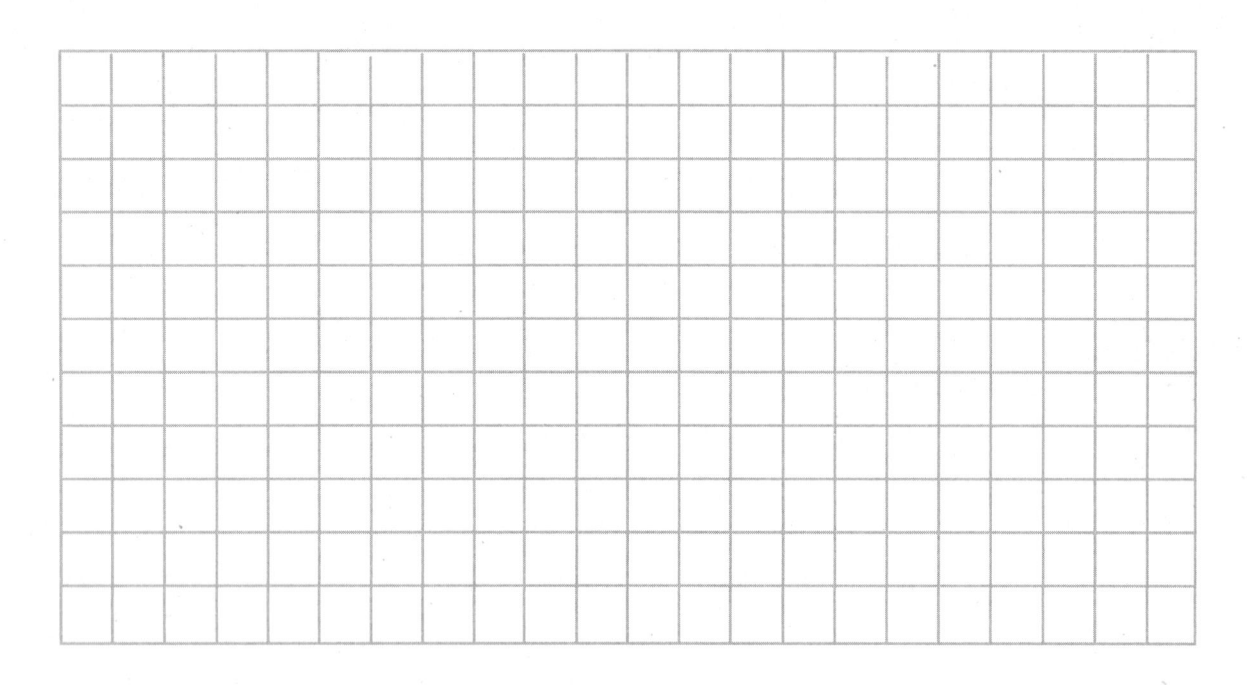

EXTRA WORKSPACE

ZEARN

Congratulations!
You completed

Grade 4 Mission 4

Construct Lines, Angles, and Shapes

Zearned it!

....
Name

....
Date

Grade 4

Mission 5

Equivalent Fractions

Lesson 2 G:4 M:5	Decompose and Group
	ZEARN STUDENT NOTES

Name:_____ Date:_____

Complete: ☐ Class:_____

1 How can you decompose $\frac{7}{8}$ into two parts?

SHOW YOUR WORK

$$\frac{7}{8} = \frac{1}{8} + \frac{1}{8} + \frac{1}{8} + \frac{1}{8} + \frac{1}{8} + \frac{1}{8} + \frac{1}{8}$$

$$\frac{7}{8} = \underline{} + \underline{}$$

EXTRA WORKSPACE

Lesson 3
G:4 M:5

Decompose and Multiply

ZEARN STUDENT NOTES

Name:_____ Date:_____

Complete: ☐ Class:_____

1 Decompose $\frac{3}{4}$ as the sum of unit fractions.

Then, express that addition sentence using multiplication.

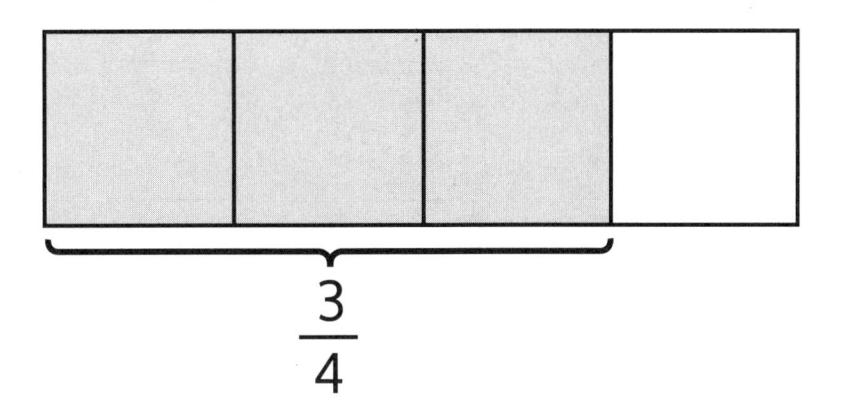

$\frac{3}{4}$

$\frac{3}{4} = \underline{} + \underline{} + \underline{}$

$\frac{3}{4} = \underline{} \times \underline{}$

EXTRA WORKSPACE

Lesson 4
G:4 M:5

Different Decompositions
ZEARN STUDENT NOTES

Name:_____ Date:_____

Complete: ☐ Class:_____

1 Use the tape diagram to show the decomposition of $\frac{1}{3}$ as the sum of smaller unit fractions.

SHOW YOUR WORK

2 Write an addition sentence and a multiplication sentence to show how many fifteenths it takes to make 1 fifth.

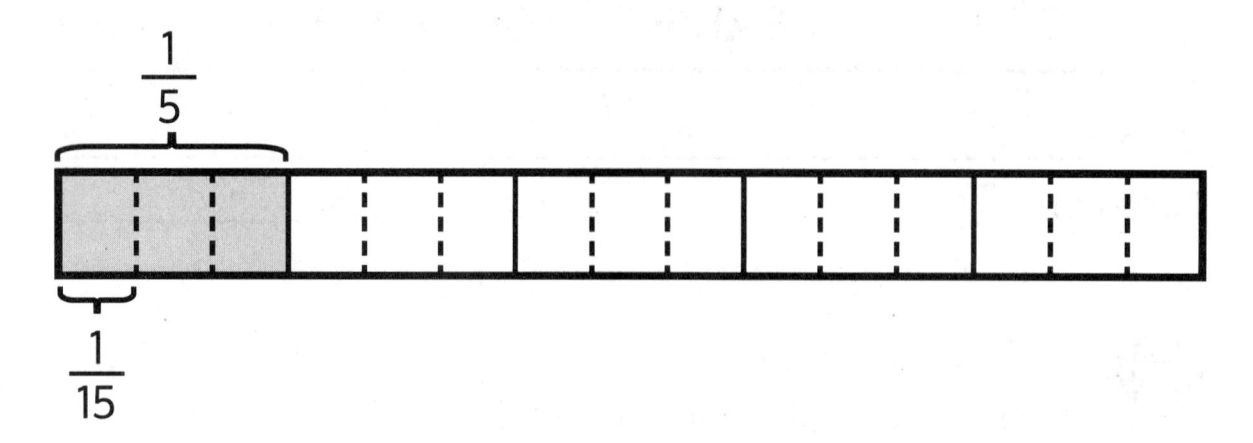

SOLVE

$\frac{1}{5}$ = ___ + ___ + ___ = ___

$\frac{1}{5}$ = ___ × ___ = ___

Lesson 6 G:4 M:5	**Area Model – Breakdown!**
	ZEARN STUDENT NOTES

Name:_____ Date:_____

Complete: ☐ Class:_____

1 Draw an area model to show that $\frac{2}{3} = \frac{8}{12}$.

SHOW YOUR WORK

2 Draw an area model to represent 5 thirds.

Then partition it into sixths to find an equivalent fraction.

SHOW YOUR WORK

$$\frac{5}{3} = \frac{}{}$$

Lesson 7
G:4 M:5

Same Area

ZEARN STUDENT NOTES

Name:_____   Date:_____

Complete: ☐   Class:_____

1 Find an equivalent fraction to $\frac{1}{4}$ that has twice as many units. Use the area model and multiplication.

Area Model:

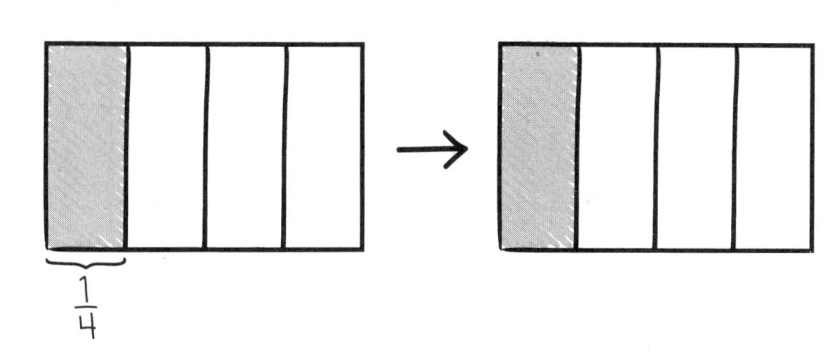

$\underbrace{}_{\frac{1}{4}}$ →

Multiplication: $\dfrac{1}{4} = \dfrac{1 \times}{4 \times} = \dfrac{}{}$

2 Rename $\frac{1}{3}$ using ninths.

Verify that the fraction you made is equivalent to $\frac{1}{3}$ by drawing an area model.

Multiplication: $\dfrac{1}{3} = \dfrac{1 \times}{3 \times} = \underline{}$

Area Model:

Lesson 8
G:4 M:5

Multiply for Equality?
ZEARN STUDENT NOTES

Name:_____ Date:_____

Complete: ☐   Class:_____

1 Use multiplication to prove that $\frac{3}{5} = \frac{6}{10}$.

Then, draw an area model to confirm your number sentence.

Multiplication: $\dfrac{3}{5} = \dfrac{3 \times}{5 \times} = \dfrac{}{}$

Area model:

141

EXTRA WORKSPACE

Lesson 9 G:4 M:5	**Same Fraction, Fewer Parts**
	ZEARN STUDENT NOTES

Name:_____ Date:_____

Complete: ☐ Class:_____

1 Compose the shaded fraction into an equivalent fraction by circling the new unit.

Then, write a division sentence based on your composition.

SHOW YOUR WORK

$$\frac{\quad}{\quad} = \frac{\quad \div \quad}{\quad \div \quad} = \frac{\quad}{\quad}$$

2 Draw area models to show $\frac{2}{6}$ and $\frac{4}{12}$.

Then, find equivalent fractions.

SHOW YOUR WORK

$\dfrac{2}{6} = \underline{\qquad}$

$\dfrac{4}{12} = \underline{\qquad}$

EXTRA WORKSPACE

Lesson 10
G:4 M:5

Same Fraction, Fewest Parts

ZEARN STUDENT NOTES

Name:_____ Date:_____

Complete: ☐   Class:_____

1 Draw an area model to represent $\frac{8}{12}$.

Then compose a fraction equivalent to $\frac{8}{12}$, with larger fractional units.

SHOW YOUR WORK

$\frac{8}{12}$

145

2 Rename $\frac{6}{12}$ with the largest units possible without using an area model.

Express the equivalence using a division number sentence.

SHOW YOUR WORK

$$\frac{6}{12} = \frac{\div }{\div } = \underline{}$$

EXTRA WORKSPACE

Lesson 13
G:4 M:5

Benchmark to Compare
ZEARN STUDENT NOTES

Name:_____   Date:_____

Complete: ☐   Class:_____

1 Compare $\frac{11}{8}$ and $\frac{10}{6}$.

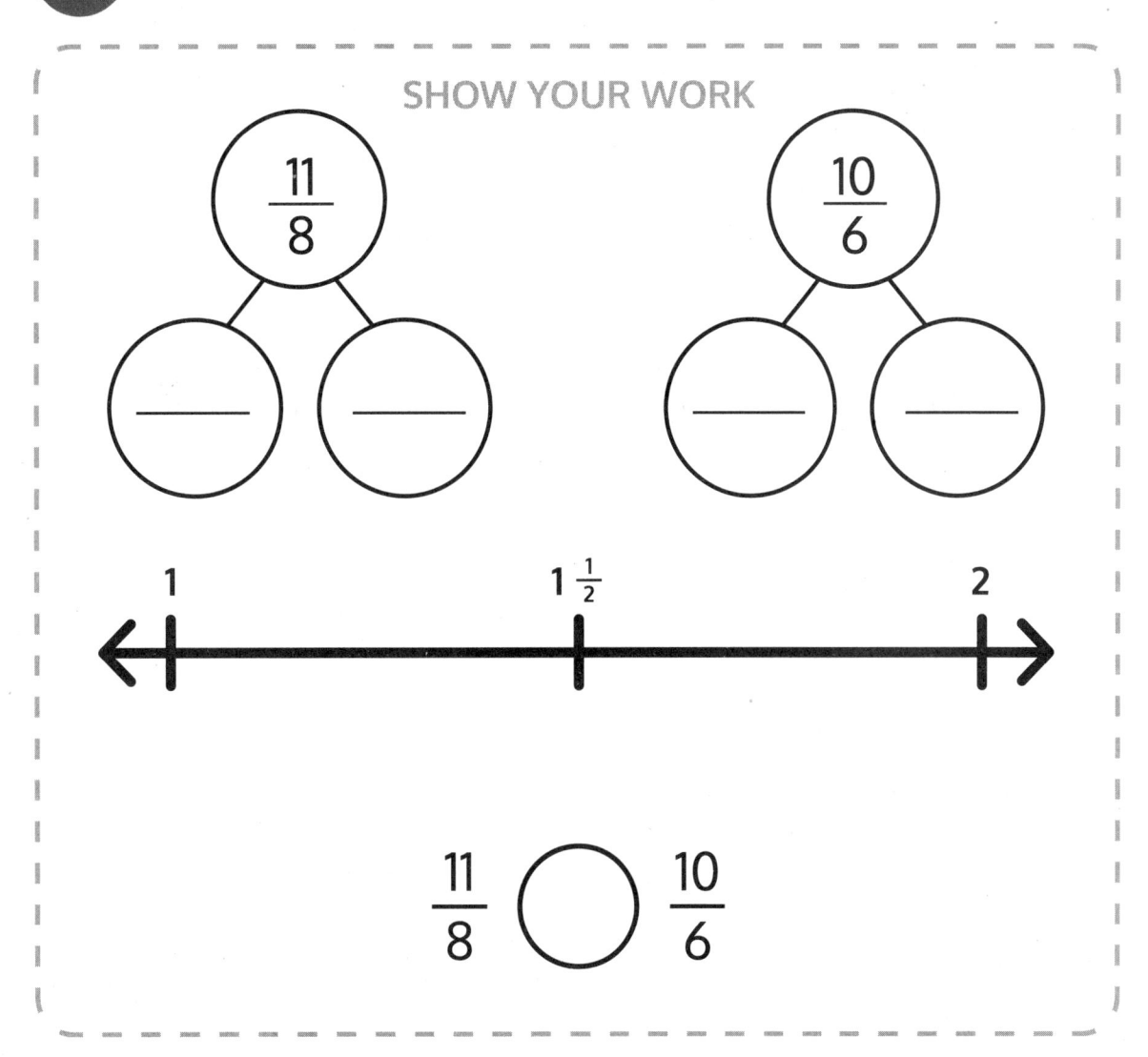

SHOW YOUR WORK

$\frac{11}{8}$

$\frac{10}{6}$

1      $1\frac{1}{2}$ 2

$\frac{11}{8}$ ◯ $\frac{10}{6}$

EXTRA WORKSPACE

Lesson 14 G:4 M:5	**Make the Same to Compare**
	ZEARN STUDENT NOTES

Name:_____ Date:_____

Complete: ☐ Class:_____

1 Use tape diagrams to model and compare $\frac{3}{5}$ and $\frac{7}{10}$.

SHOW YOUR WORK

$\frac{3}{5}$ [ ] $\frac{3 \times}{5 \times}$ = ___

$\frac{7}{10}$ [ ]

Common denominator: ___ ◯ ___

$\frac{3}{5}$ ◯ $\frac{7}{10}$

EXTRA WORKSPACE

Lesson 16 G:4 M:5	**Like Units Make It Work**
	ZEARN STUDENT NOTES

Name:_____ Date:_____

Complete: ☐ Class:_____

1 5 sixths − 4 sixths = _____

SHOW YOUR WORK

$\longleftrightarrow$

_____ − _____ = _____

151

EXTRA WORKSPACE

Lesson 17
G:4 M:5

Whole Use
ZEARN STUDENT NOTES

Name:_____ Date:_____

Complete: ☐ Class:_____

1 Solve $1\frac{1}{4} - \frac{3}{4}$.

SHOW YOUR WORK

$1\frac{1}{4}$

$1\frac{1}{4} = \underline{\qquad} + \underline{\qquad} = \underline{\qquad}$

1

$1\frac{1}{4} - \frac{3}{4} = \underline{\qquad}$

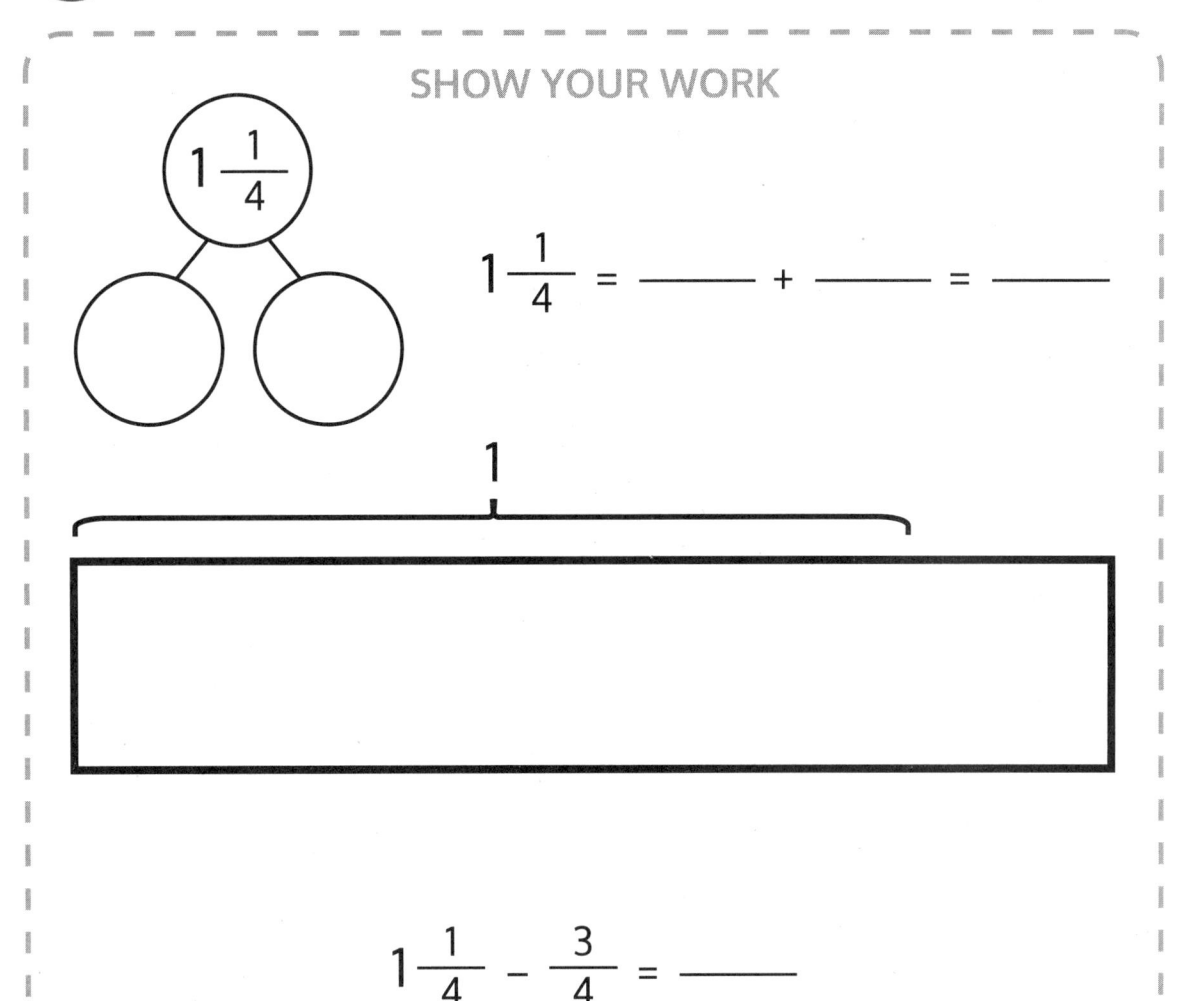

153

EXTRA WORKSPACE

Lesson 18
G:4 M:5

Three's Company
ZEARN STUDENT NOTES

Name:_____   Date:_____

Complete: ☐   Class:_____

1) $\dfrac{1}{6} + \dfrac{4}{6} + \dfrac{2}{6}$

SHOW YOUR WORK

2 Mrs. Cashmore bought a melon that weighed $1\frac{3}{5}$ pounds. She cut a piece that weighed $\frac{4}{5}$ pound and gave it to her neighbor. She then had $\frac{1}{5}$ pound as a snack.

How much of the melon is left?

DRAW

SOLVE

Lesson 20
G:4 M:5

Like Units, Like Sum
ZEARN STUDENT NOTES

Name:_____ Date:_____

Complete: ☐ Class:_____

1 $\frac{1}{2} + \frac{1}{8}$. Use the tape diagrams to help you solve.

SHOW YOUR WORK

$\frac{1}{2}$ [   ]

$\frac{1}{8}$ [   ]

$\frac{1}{2} + \frac{1}{8} =$ ____ + ____ = ____

157

EXTRA WORKSPACE

Lesson 21
G:4 M:5

Sum It Up
ZEARN STUDENT NOTES

Name:_____ Date:_____

Complete: ☐   Class:_____

1 Draw a number bond to show $\frac{9}{6}$ as a whole and parts.

Then, use your number bond to write $\frac{9}{6}$ as a mixed number.

SHOW YOUR WORK

$\frac{9}{6}$ = _____ + _____ = _____

EXTRA WORKSPACE

Lesson 22
G:4 M:5

Fraction To/Fraction From
ZEARN STUDENT NOTES

Name:_____ Date:_____

Complete: ☐   Class:_____

1 Draw a tape diagram to represent $2 + \frac{1}{2}$.

$2 + \frac{1}{2} =$ _____

2 Draw a tape diagram to represent $3 - \frac{1}{4}$.

$3 - \frac{1}{4} =$ _____

3 Solve $7 - \frac{3}{5}$ using a number bond. Then, use the number line to represent your number sentence.

SHOW YOUR WORK

$7 - \frac{3}{5} =$ _____

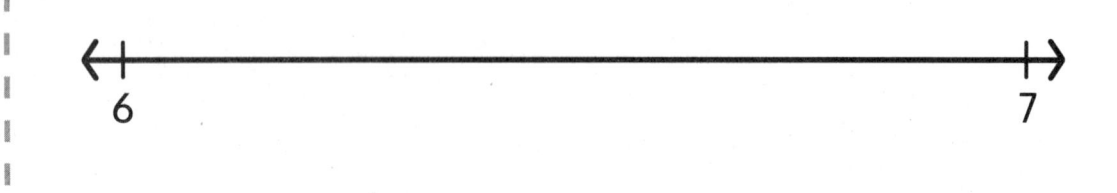

_____ _____

6 ⟵——————————————⟶ 7

EXTRA WORKSPACE

Lesson 23
G:4 M:5

Fraction Build-up
ZEARN STUDENT NOTES

Name:_____ Date:_____

Complete: ☐ Class:_____

1 Show that $10 \times \frac{1}{5} = 2 \times \frac{5}{5} = 2$ on the number line.

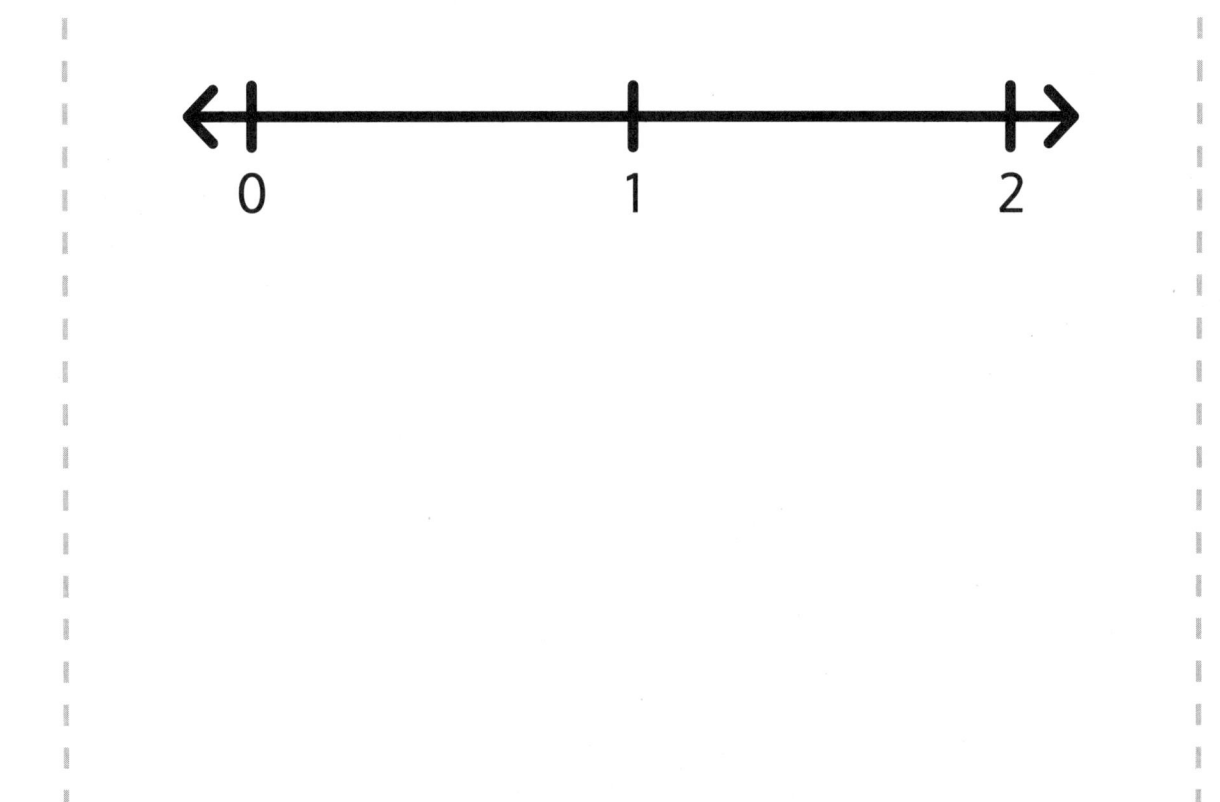

SHOW YOUR WORK

<--|---------|---------|-->
0   1   2

2 Multiply $8 \times \frac{1}{3}$ and write the product as a mixed number. Draw a number line to support your answer.

$8 \times \frac{1}{3} = $ _____

NUMBER LINE

EXTRA WORKSPACE

Lesson 25
G:4 M:5

Form Follows Function
ZEARN STUDENT NOTES

Name:_____ Date:_____

Complete: ☐ Class:_____

1. On the number line, show how many sixths it takes to go from 0 to $2\frac{1}{6}$.

<-|-|-|-|-|-|-|-|-|-|-|-|-|-|-|-|-|-|-|->
0   1   2   3

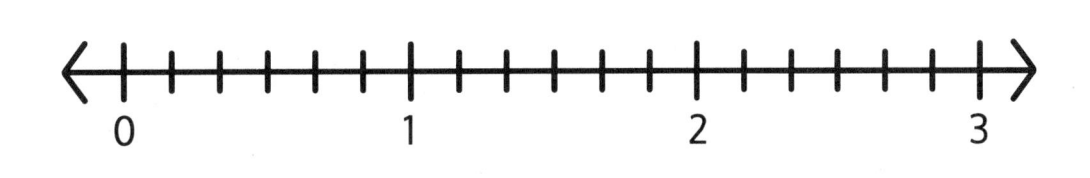

2. Convert $2\frac{2}{3}$ into a fraction greater than 1 using multiplication.

$$2\frac{2}{3} = (\underline{\qquad} \times \underline{\qquad}) + \frac{2}{3}$$

$$= \underline{\qquad} + \underline{\qquad}$$

$$= \underline{\qquad}$$

EXTRA WORKSPACE

Lesson 26
G:4 M:5

Benchmark Boogie
ZEARN STUDENT NOTES

Name:_____   Date:_____

Complete: ☐   Class:_____

1 Convert $\frac{43}{8}$ and $\frac{35}{6}$ to mixed numbers and compare them.

SHOW YOUR WORK

$\frac{43}{8}$ = _____ $\frac{35}{6}$ = _____

____ ◯ $\frac{1}{2}$ ____ ◯ $\frac{1}{2}$

_____ ◯ _____

167

EXTRA WORKSPACE

Lesson 27
G:4 M:5

We Like Units
ZEARN STUDENT NOTES

Name:_____ Date:_____

Complete: ☐ Class:_____

1 Draw tape diagrams of $\frac{2}{6}$ and $\frac{3}{12}$ to compare $2\frac{2}{6}$ and $2\frac{3}{12}$.

Which number is bigger?

SHOW YOUR WORK

$\frac{2}{6}$

$\frac{3}{12}$

Common denominator: ____ ◯ ____

$2\frac{2}{6}$ ◯ $2\frac{3}{12}$

EXTRA WORKSPACE

Lesson 28 G:4 M:5	**Spotting and Plotting**
	ZEARN STUDENT NOTES

Name:_____ Date:_____

Complete: ☐   Class:_____

1 Mr. O'Neil's science class is growing sunflowers. The table and line plot show how tall each plant grew.

What is the height difference between the tallest and shortest plant?

Height of Sunflower Plants (Inches)

$55\frac{1}{2}$	58	$58\frac{1}{2}$	59
58	$59\frac{1}{2}$	$57\frac{1}{2}$	$56\frac{1}{2}$
$57\frac{1}{2}$	$58\frac{1}{2}$	59	58

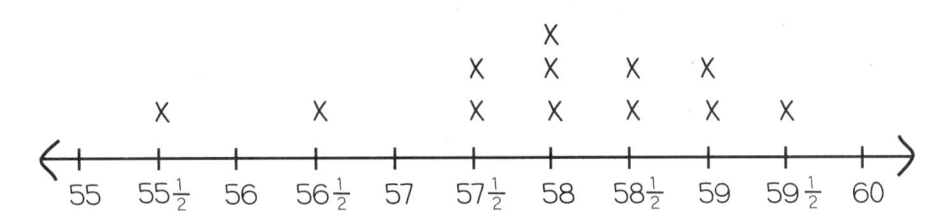

```
                                    X
                              X     X     X     X
         X           X        X  X  X  X  X
    <----+----+----+----+----+----+----+----+----+----+---->
        55  55½  56  56½  57  57½  58  58½  59  59½  60
```

x = 1 sunflower plant

SOLVE

2 The chart shows the distance fourth-graders in Ms. Smith's class were able to run without stopping.

Create a line plot to display the data in the table.

Then, use the line plot to answer: How much further did Jack run than Arianna?

Student	Distance (miles)
Joe	$2\frac{3}{4}$
Arianna	$1\frac{3}{4}$
Bobbi	$2\frac{1}{4}$
Morgan	$1\frac{1}{2}$
Jack	$2\frac{1}{2}$
Saisha	$2\frac{1}{4}$
Tyler	$2\frac{2}{4}$
Jenny	$\frac{2}{4}$
Anson	$\frac{4}{4}$
Chandra	$\frac{4}{2}$

SOLVE

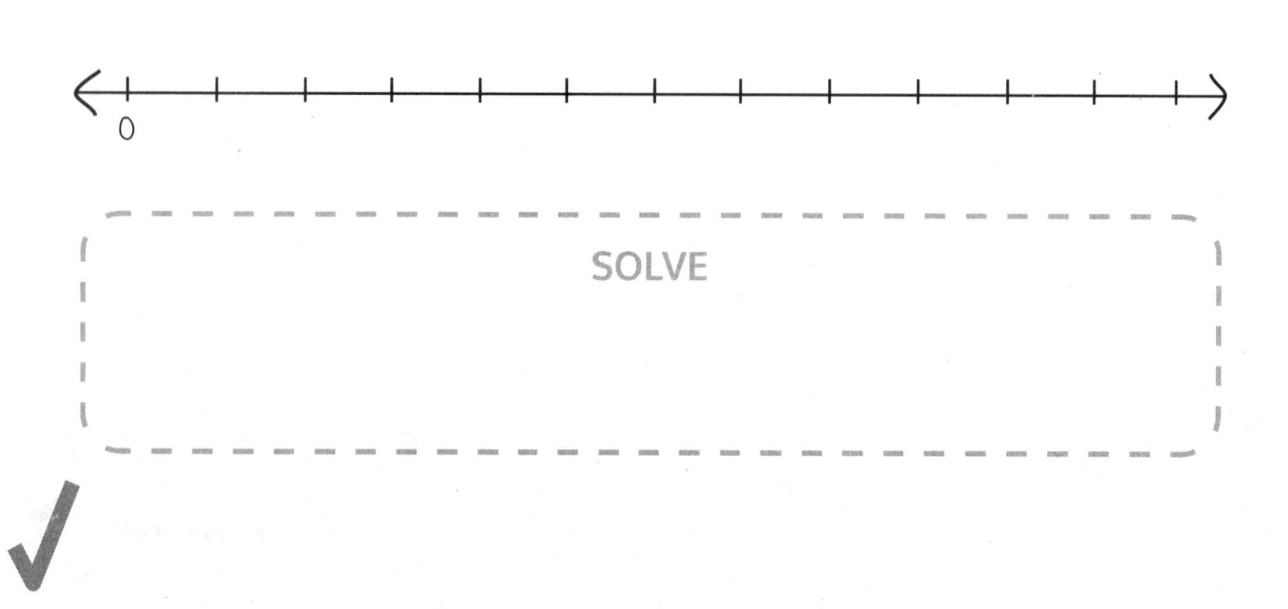

Lesson 30
G:4 M:5

Sum Mixed, Sum Not
ZEARN STUDENT NOTES

Name:_____ Date:_____

Complete: ☐ Class:_____

1 How much do we need to add to $3\frac{1}{8}$ to make a whole?

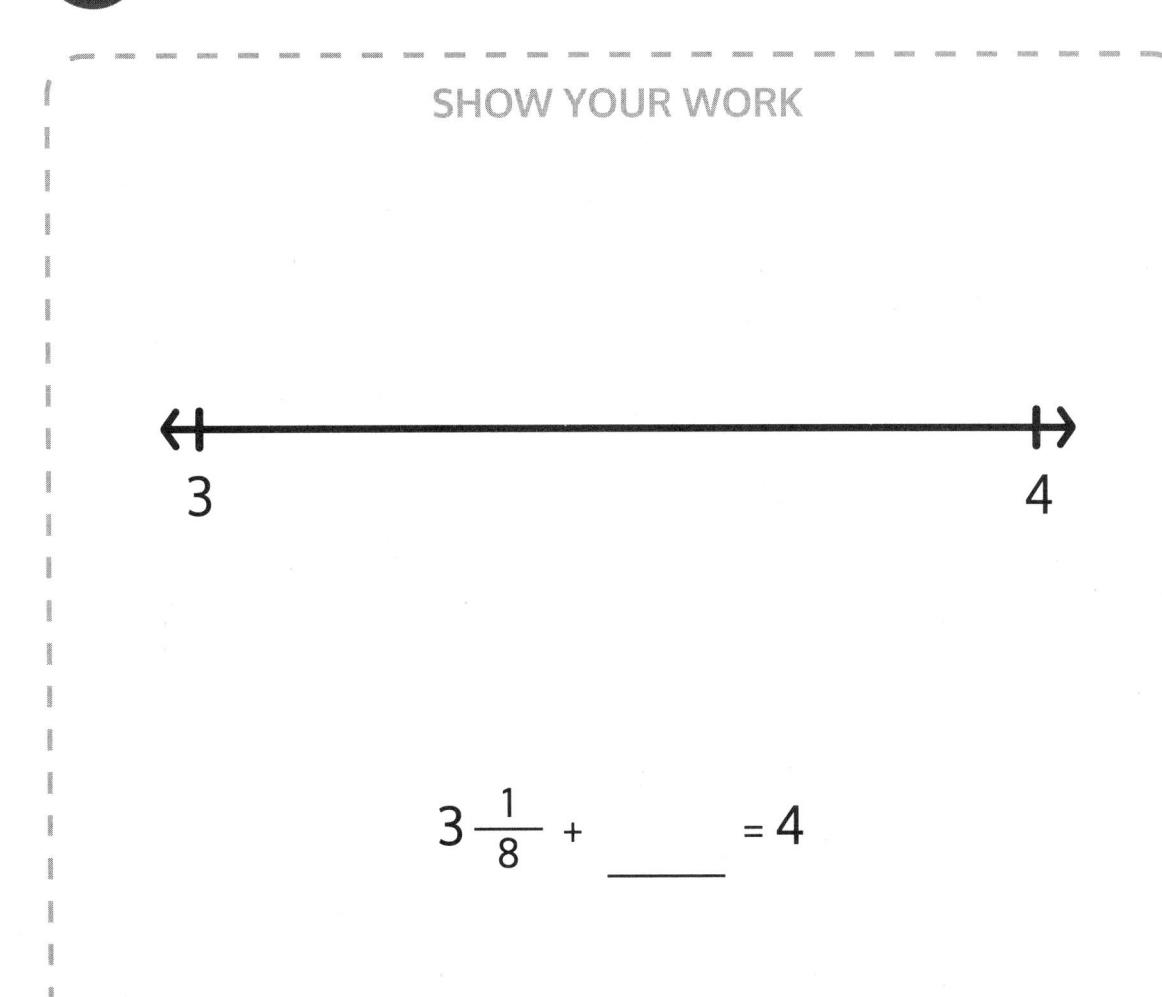

SHOW YOUR WORK

←|―――――――――――|→
3   4

$3\frac{1}{8} + \underline{} = 4$

173

EXTRA WORKSPACE

Lesson 31 G:4 M:5	**Mixed Sums**
	ZEARN STUDENT NOTES

Name:_____ Date:_____

Complete: ☐ Class:_____

1 Solve by adding like units.

SHOW YOUR WORK

$4\frac{2}{3} + 3\frac{1}{3} + 5\frac{2}{3} =$

EXTRA WORKSPACE

Lesson 32
G:4 M:5

Count Back to Subtract
ZEARN STUDENT NOTES

Name:_____ Date:_____

Complete: ☐ Class:_____

1 Solve by decomposing and subtracting.

SHOW YOUR WORK

$4\frac{1}{5} - \frac{3}{5} =$ _____

$\frac{1}{5}$ ____

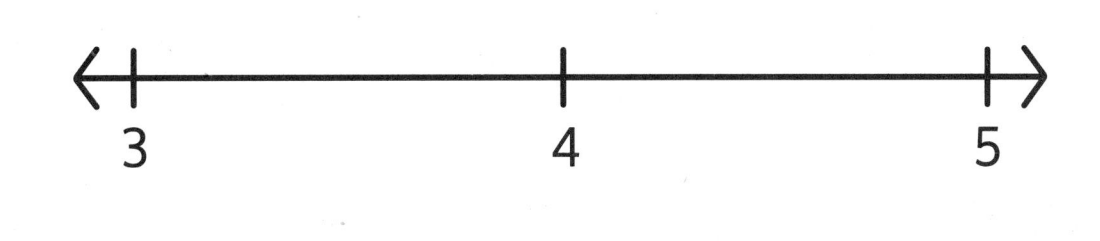

⟵|—————————|—————————|⟶
3   4   5

177

EXTRA WORKSPACE

Lesson 33
G:4 M:5

Break Down to Subtract

ZEARN STUDENT NOTES

Name:_____ Date:_____

Complete: ☐ Class:_____

1 Solve by subtracting like units.

SHOW YOUR WORK

$$10\frac{1}{5} - 1\frac{3}{5} =$$

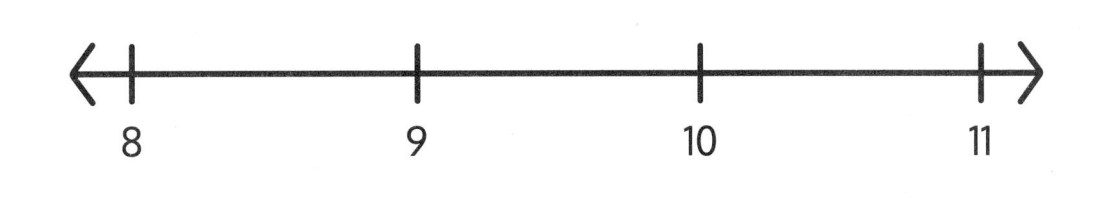

```
<----|--------|--------|--------|---->
     8        9       10       11
```

EXTRA WORKSPACE

Lesson 35 G:4 M:5	Associate How You Like
	ZEARN STUDENT NOTES

Name:_____   Date:_____

Complete: ☐   Class:_____

1 Solve numerically and using unit form.

SHOW YOUR WORK

$$5 \times \frac{3}{4}$$

EXTRA WORKSPACE

Lesson 36 G:4 M:5	**Fast Times**
	ZEARN STUDENT NOTES

Name:_____ Date:_____

Complete: ☐ Class:_____

1 Rhonda exercised for $\frac{5}{6}$ hour every day for 5 days. How many total hours did Rhonda exercise?

DRAW

SOLVE

She exercised _____ hours in 5 days.

2 Six friends each drank $\frac{2}{3}$ cup of juice.

If a bottle of juice contains 3 cups, how many bottles of juice were needed?

DRAW

SOLVE

The friends drank _____ cups.

_____ bottles of juice were needed.

Lesson 37 G:4 M:5	Multiply Mix
	ZEARN STUDENT NOTES

Name:_____ Date:_____

Complete: ☐   Class:_____

1 Draw a tape diagram showing $3\frac{1}{5}$. Then, draw another copy of the tape diagram.

Use your drawing to solve $2 \times 3\frac{1}{5}$.

DRAW

SOLVE

$2 \times 3\frac{1}{5} = ($ _____ × _____ $) + ($ _____ × _____ $)$

= _____ + _____

= _____

185

2 In April, Jenny ran in a marathon as part of a relay team. She ran $6\frac{55}{100}$ miles. In September, Jenny ran 4 times as far to complete a marathon on her own.

How far did Jenny run in September?

DRAW

SOLVE

Lesson 39 G:4 M:5	**Prepare to Compare**
	ZEARN STUDENT NOTES

Name:_____ Date:_____

Complete: ☐ Class:_____

1 Natasha's sculpture was $5\frac{2}{10}$ inches tall. Maya's sculpture was 4 times as tall.

How much taller was Maya's sculpture than Natasha's?

DRAW | SOLVE

Maya's sculpture was _____ inches taller than Natasha's sculpture.

EXTRA WORKSPACE

Lesson 40
G:4 M:5

Plotting Along
ZEARN STUDENT NOTES

Name:_____ Date:_____

Complete: ☐ Class:_____

1 The chart shows the yearly rainfall for Boulder, Colorado. Use the data to create a line plot.

What is the difference in rainfall between the wettest and driest years?

Year	Rainfall (meters)
2007	$2\frac{4}{6}$
2008	$2\frac{1}{3}$
2009	$1\frac{4}{6}$
2010	$2\frac{2}{3}$
2011	$2\frac{3}{6}$
2012	$1\frac{2}{6}$
2013	$1\frac{2}{3}$
2014	$2\frac{5}{6}$

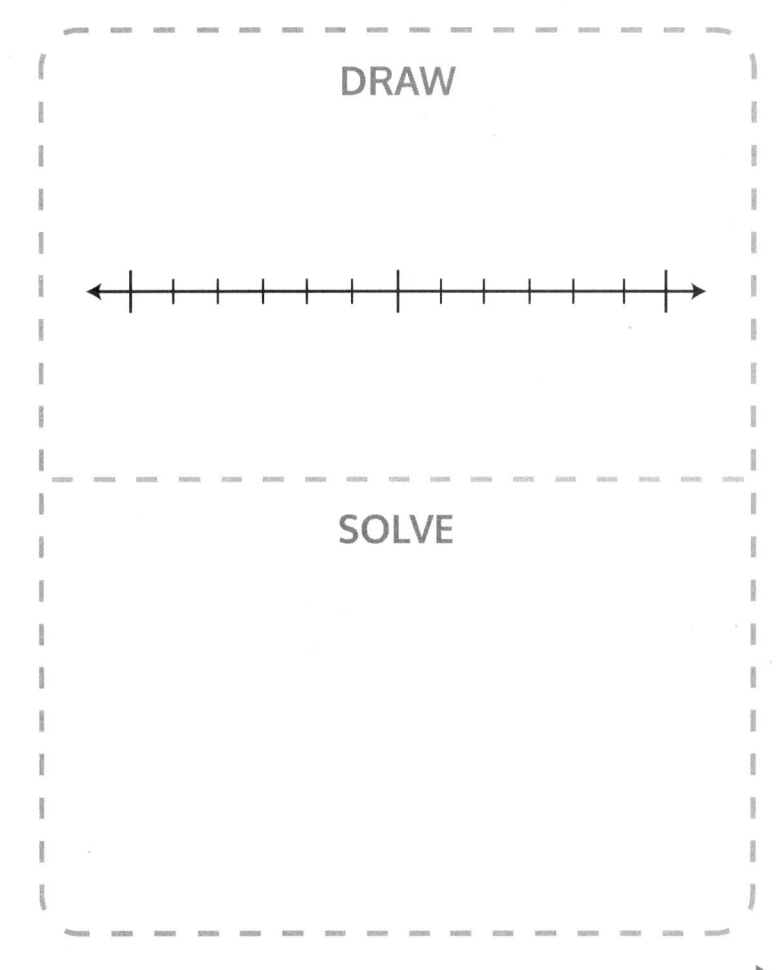

DRAW

SOLVE

2 In which year did it rain twice as much as 2012?

SHOW YOUR WORK

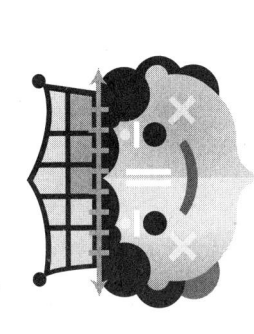

Congratulations!
You completed

Grade 4 Mission 5
Equivalent Fractions

Zearned it!

Name

Date

Grade 4

Mission 6
Decimal Fractions

Lesson 2 G:4 M:6	Shaded Fractions, Shaded Decimals
	ZEARN STUDENT NOTES

Name:_____ Date:_____

Complete: ☐   Class:_____

You will need a centimeter ruler for this lesson.

1 Using the centimeter ruler, draw a line that measures 2 cm. Then, extend the line by $\frac{6}{10}$ cm.

DRAW

SOLVE

Fraction equation: _____ cm + _____ cm = _____ cm

Decimal equation: _____ cm + _____ cm = _____ cm

2 Shade to represent $3\frac{2}{10}$ using the area models.

SHOW YOUR WORK

1   1   1   1

Decimal equation: _____ = _____ + _____

We need _____ more to make 4 wholes.

EXTRA WORKSPACE

Lesson 3
G:4 M:6

Equivalence Extravaganza
ZEARN STUDENT NOTES

Name:_____ Date:_____

Complete: ☐ Class:_____

1 Write the value represented by these place value disks in unit form and standard form. Then solve.

(10) (10) (10) (10)   (1) (1)   (0.1) (0.1) (0.1) (0.1) (0.1) (0.1)

↓   ↓   ↓
____tens   +   ____ones   +   ____tenths
↓   ↓   ↓
____   +   ____   +   ____   =   ____

                                    =   ____

197

EXTRA WORKSPACE

Lesson 4
G:4 M:6

From Tenths to Hundredths
ZEARN STUDENT NOTES

Name:_____ Date:_____

Complete: ☐ Class:_____

1 Shade in the amount shown. Then, write the equivalent decimal.

SHOW YOUR WORK

$\frac{5}{10}$ m = _____ m

1 meter

199

EXTRA WORKSPACE

Lesson 6 G:4 M:6	Zoom! Plot!
	ZEARN STUDENT NOTES

Name:_____   Date:_____

Complete: ☐   Class:_____

1 Show $3\frac{46}{100}$ on the number line.

SHOW YOUR WORK

$3\frac{46}{100}$

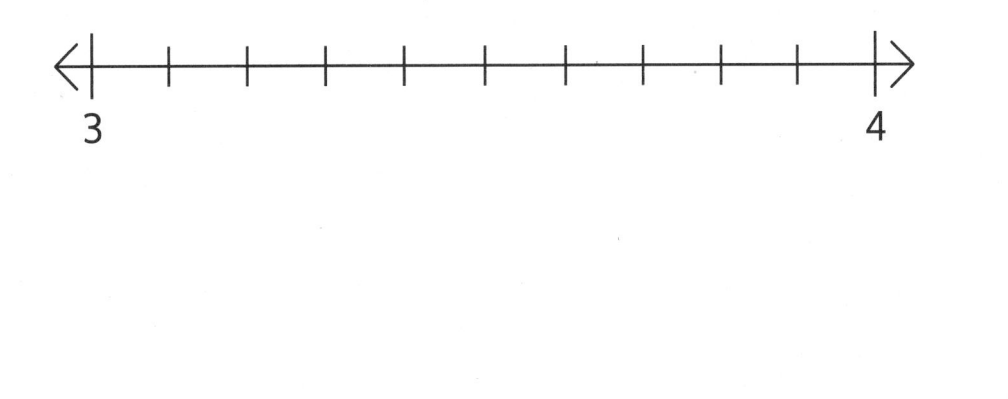

3 — — — — — — — — — — 4

EXTRA WORKSPACE

Lesson 7
G:4 M:6

Expand
ZEARN STUDENT NOTES

Name:_____ Date:_____

Complete: ☐ Class:_____

1. Write 340.83 in expanded form using fraction notation and decimal notation.

FRACTION NOTATION

DECIMAL NOTATION

203

EXTRA WORKSPACE

| Lesson 9 | PVC, Easy as 0.1, 0.2, 0.3 |
| G:4 M:6 | ZEARN STUDENT NOTES |

Name:_____ Date:_____

Complete: ☐ Class:_____

1 Shade the tape diagrams to represent the length of each shaded meter stick. Then, write a sentence to compare the lengths.

B
0.41 m

G
0.35 m

	ones (meters)	tenths	hundredths
B			
G			

Tape _____ is longer than tape _____ because

_____ meters is longer than _____ meters.

2 Record the weight of each object in the place value chart. Then, find the lightest object.

	ones	tenths	hundredths
Orange			
Apple			
Book			

The _____ weighs less than the _____

and the _____.

---

3 Record the volume of each graduated cylinder in the place value chart. Then, order the cylinders from least volume to greatest volume.

	ones	tenths	hundredths
A			
B			
C			
D			

_____

Lesson 12
G:4 M:6

Add Your Understanding
ZEARN STUDENT NOTES

Name:_____ Date:_____

Complete: ☐ Class:_____

1 Solve $\frac{3}{4} + \frac{1}{2}$.

SHOW YOUR WORK

2 Solve $\frac{6}{10} + \frac{57}{100}$.

Write your answer as a decimal.

SHOW YOUR WORK

3 Model $\frac{9}{10} + \frac{64}{100}$ using the area models.

Then, solve and write your final answer as a decimal.

SHOW YOUR WORK

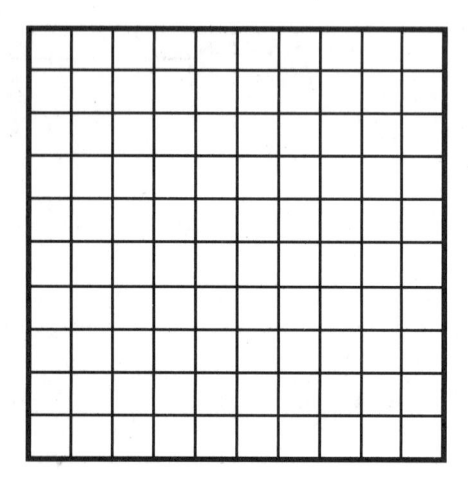

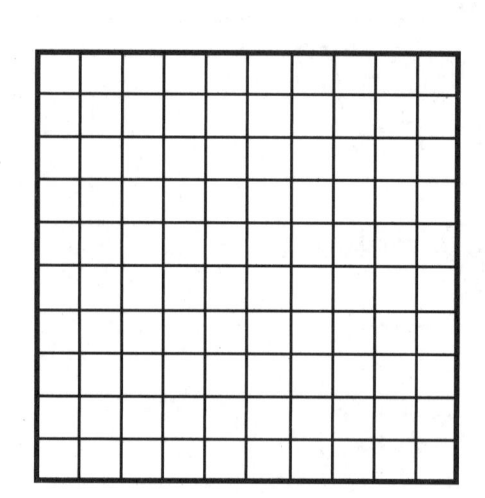

Lesson 13
G:4 M:6

Decimal + Decimal
ZEARN STUDENT NOTES

Name:_____ Date:_____

Complete: ☐ Class:_____

1 Solve 0.30 + 0.5

Express your answer as a decimal number.

SHOW YOUR WORK

2 Rewrite 5.6 + 4.53 as the sum of two mixed numbers. Solve. Then, rewrite your number sentence in decimal form.

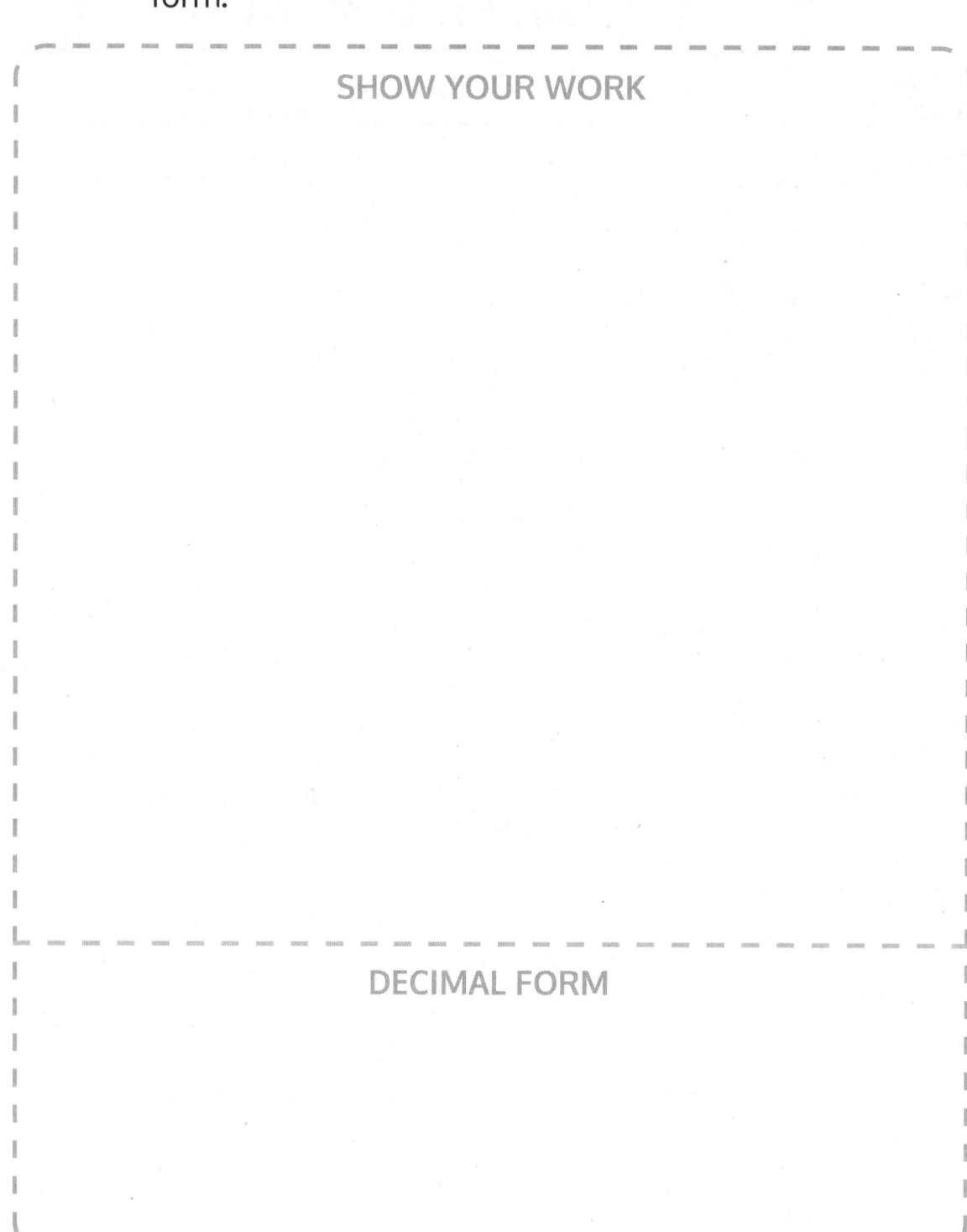

SHOW YOUR WORK

DECIMAL FORM

Lesson 14
G:4 M:6

For Good Measure
ZEARN STUDENT NOTES

Name:_____ Date:_____

Complete: ☐ Class:_____

1 A team of three friends ran a relay race. Camille ran the fastest, measuring 29.2 seconds. Marco was 1.89 seconds slower than Camille. Laina ran 0.9 seconds slower than Marco.

What was the team's total time for the race?

DRAW

SOLVE

The team's total was _____ seconds.

EXTRA WORKSPACE

Lesson 15
G:4 M:6

Money, Money, Money!
ZEARN STUDENT NOTES

Name: _____ Date: _____

Complete: ☐ Class: _____

1 Give the total amount of money in fraction and decimal form.

3 quarters and 4 dimes

SHOW YOUR WORK

Fraction: _____   Mixed Number: _____

Decimal: _____

EXTRA WORKSPACE

Lesson 16
G:4 M:6

Mo' Money, Mo' Math

ZEARN STUDENT NOTES

Name:_____ Date:_____

Complete: ☐   Class:_____

1 Jose wants to buy a pen for $2.70, a box of pencils for $3.39 and an eraser for $1.86.

How much will he spend in total?

DRAW

SOLVE

Jose will spend _____ .

2 Jose has 6 ones, 3 quarters, 2 dimes, and 9 pennies.

Is that enough money to buy the pen, box of pencils, and eraser?

SHOW YOUR WORK

EXTRA WORKSPACE

ZEARN

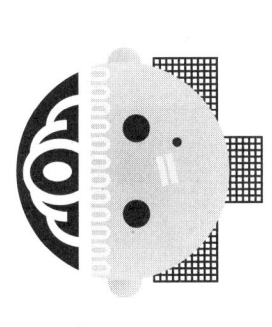

Congratulations!
You completed

Grade 4 Mission 6
Decimal Fractions

Zearned it!

Name .... Date ....

Grade 4

Mission 7

Multiply and Measure

Lesson 1
G:4 M:7

Conversion Counts
ZEARN STUDENT NOTES

Name:_____ Date:_____

Complete: ☐ Class:_____

1 Complete the pounds to ounces conversion table.

Pounds	Ounces
1	
2	
3	
4	
5	
6	
7	
8	
9	
10	

SHOW YOUR WORK

15 pounds = _____ ounces

221

2 Complete the yards to feet conversion table.

Yards	Feet
1	
2	
3	
4	
5	
6	
7	
8	
9	
10	

EXTRA WORKSPACE

3 Complete the feet to inches conversion table.

Feet	Inches
1	
2	
3	
4	
5	
6	
7	
8	
9	
10	

EXTRA WORKSPACE

Lesson 2
G:4 M:7

Conversion Rules

ZEARN STUDENT NOTES

Name:_____ Date:_____

Complete: ☐ Class:_____

1 Use the tape diagrams to help you complete the chart. Then, use the chart to fill in the blanks.

1 gallon

1 quart

1 pint

1 cup

Gallons	Quarts	Pints	Cups
		1	2
	1	2	4
1	_____	_____	_____

SHOW YOUR WORK

1 gallon = _____ quarts = _____ pints = _____ cups

2 Brandon made 5 gallons of lemonade for his party.

How many cups of lemonade can he serve? Use a tape diagram to help you solve.

DRAW

SOLVE

Lesson 3
G:4 M:7

Conversion Time
ZEARN STUDENT NOTES

Name:_____ Date:_____

Complete: ☐ Class:_____

1 Complete the minutes to seconds conversion table.

Find the number of seconds in 16 minutes.

Minutes	Seconds
1	
2	
3	
4	
5	
6	
7	
8	
9	
10	

SHOW YOUR WORK

16 minutes equals _____ seconds.

2 Complete the hours to minutes conversion table.

Hours	Minutes
1	
2	
3	
4	
5	
6	
7	
8	
9	
10	

3 Complete the days to hours conversion table.

Days	Hours
1	
2	
3	
4	
5	
6	
7	
8	
9	
10	

4 The Apollo 17 mission was completed in 12 days, 14 hours.

How many hours did the mission last?

SHOW YOUR WORK

The Apollo 17 mission lasted _____ hours.

Lesson 4
G:4 M:7

Conversion Immersion
ZEARN STUDENT NOTES

Name:_____ Date:_____

Complete: ☐ Class:_____

1 Ayla spent 4 hours 18 minutes on a bus from Chicago to St. Louis.

How many minutes was the bus ride?

1 hr = 60 min

DRAW

SOLVE

2 Daniel built a block tower that was 5 yards tall. The school record was 14 feet.

Did Daniel beat the record?

1 yd = 3 ft

DRAW

SOLVE

_____

_____

EXTRA WORKSPACE

Lesson 6
G:4 M:7

Mixed Unit Strategies
ZEARN STUDENT NOTES

Name:_____ Date:_____

Complete: ☐ Class:_____

1 Solve by counting up or adding like units.

1 gal = 4 qt

SHOW YOUR WORK

5 gal 2 qt + 4 gal 3 qt = _____

2 Solve.

1 qt = 4 c

SHOW YOUR WORK

8 qt 1 c − 6 qt 3 c = _____

EXTRA WORKSPACE

Lesson 7
G:4 M:7

Inch to Foot, Feet to Yards
ZEARN STUDENT NOTES

Name:_____ Date:_____

Complete: ☐ Class:_____

1 Express 9 feet 8 inches + 7 inches in feet and inches.

1 ft = 12 in

SHOW YOUR WORK

9 ft 8 in + 7 in = _____ ft _____ in

2 Express 7 feet 4 inches − 5 feet 9 inches in feet and inches.

1 ft = 12 in

SHOW YOUR WORK

7 ft 4 in − 5 ft 9 in = _____ ft _____ in

EXTRA WORKSPACE

Lesson 10
G:4 M:7

Minutes and Miles

ZEARN STUDENT NOTES

Name:_____ Date:_____

Complete: ☐ Class:_____

1 Paula's time swimming in the triathlon was 1 hour 25 minutes. Her time biking was 5 hours longer than her swimming time. She ran for 4 hours 50 minutes.

How long did it take her to complete all three parts of the race?

1 hr = 60 min

DRAW

SOLVE

It took Paula _____ hrs _____ mins to finish the race.

EXTRA WORKSPACE

Lesson 11
G:4 M:7

Multi-Step Measure
ZEARN STUDENT NOTES

Name:_____ Date:_____

Complete: ☐   Class:_____

1 Chef Joe has 8 pounds 4 ounces of beans in his freezer. This is one third of the beans needed to make the number of burritos he needs for a party.

If he uses 4 ounces of beans for each burrito, how many burritos is he planning to make?

1 lb = 16 oz

DRAW

SOLVE

Chef Joe is planning on making _____ burritos.

2 Sarah read for 1 hour, 12 minutes over the weekend. It took her 3 minutes to read one page.

How many pages did she read?

1 hr = 60 min

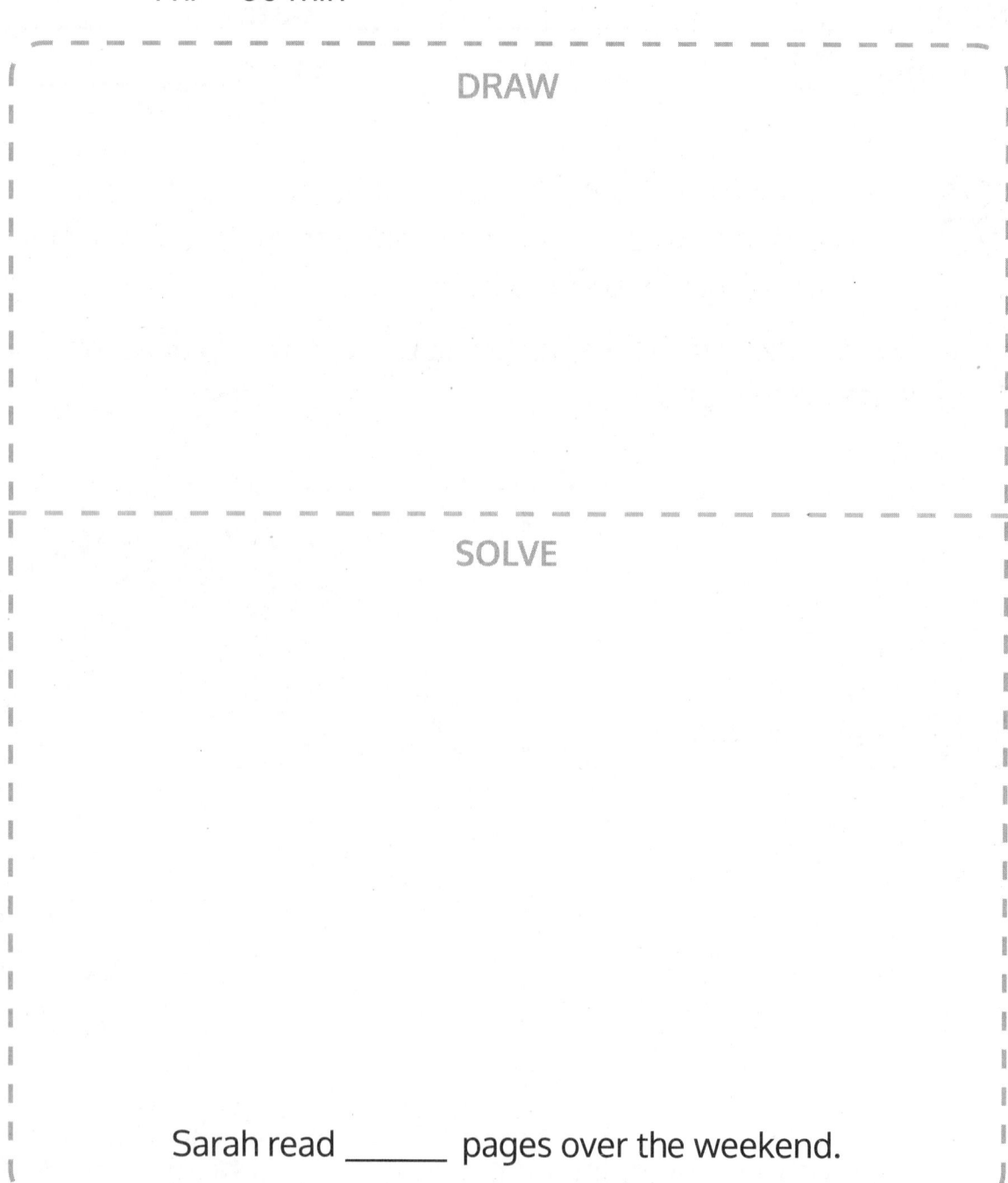

DRAW

SOLVE

Sarah read _____ pages over the weekend.

Lesson 12
G:4 M:7

Action Fraction Units
ZEARN STUDENT NOTES

Name:_____ Date:_____

Complete: ☐ Class:_____

1 Use a tape diagram to convert feet to yards.

_____ yd = 1 ft

_____ yd = 2 ft

2 Draw a tape diagram to show 4 quarts equals 1 gallon. Shade $\frac{1}{4}$ of your tape diagram.

SHOW YOUR WORK

3 How many inches are in $2\frac{1}{2}$ feet?

1 ft = 12 in

SHOW YOUR WORK

$2\frac{1}{2}$ feet = _____ inches.

EXTRA WORKSPACE

Lesson 13
G:4 M:7

Conversion Continued
ZEARN STUDENT NOTES

Name:_____ Date:_____

Complete: ☐ Class:_____

1 Use a tape diagram to convert $\frac{1}{16}$ pound to ounces.

1 pound = 16 ounces

SHOW YOUR WORK

$\frac{1}{16}$ pound = _____ ounce

2 Label the tape diagram to show that $2\frac{1}{2}$ pounds = 40 ounces.

1 pound = 16 ounces

239

3 Find the number of minutes in $3\frac{1}{2}$ hours.

1 hour = 60 minutes

SHOW YOUR WORK

There are _____ minutes in $3\frac{1}{2}$ hours.

EXTRA WORKSPACE

Lesson 14
G:4 M:7

Convert-a-rama!
ZEARN STUDENT NOTES

Name:_____ Date:_____

Complete: ☐ Class:_____

1 A flamingo is $4\frac{1}{4}$ feet tall. A giraffe's height is 3 times that of the flamingo.

How much taller is the giraffe than the flamingo? Give your answer in feet and inches.

1 ft = 12 in

DRAW

SOLVE

The giraffe is _____ ft _____ in taller than the flamingo.

EXTRA WORKSPACE

ZEARN

Congratulations!
You completed

Grade 4 Mission 7
Multiply and Measure

Zearned it!

Name

Date

EXTRA WORKSPACE

EXTRA WORKSPACE

EXTRA WORKSPACE

EXTRA WORKSPACE